Pater ipse colendi
haud facilem esse viam voluit

VIRGIL, G. 1, 121

A MANUAL OF HOME
Vegetable Gardening

BY FRANCIS C. COULTER

Illustrated by **TABEA HOFMANN**

DOVER PUBLICATIONS, INC.
NEW YORK

This Dover edition, first published in 1973, is a republication of the work originally published in 1942 by Doubleday, Doran & Company, Inc. This edition is unabridged and unaltered, except that a two-page foreword by Richardson Wright has been omitted because it is out of date.

International Standard Book Number: 0-486-22945-9
Library of Congress Catalog Card Number: 73-77631

Manufactured in the United States of America
Dover Publications, Inc.
180 Varick Street
New York, N. Y. 10014

Contents

I know well enough that all Books of Gardening have usually begun with a Preface full of the praises given to it, and that consequently it may be thought this ought to begin so too. But since I am far from presuming myself to say anything new that may at all enhance the Esteem which is due to *Gardens*, or to the *Art* that teaches their Construction, and therefore cannot but think it very impertinent to go about to persuade anyone to study it; when I observe the most part of Men possess'd with a natural passion for so sweet and profitable an Occupation, I shall waive those Compliments, and fall down right upon the pursuit of my Design, which is to instruct, in case I can show myself really master enough of the *Art* worthily to perform it.

JEAN DE LA QUINTINYE, 1690

A MANUAL OF HOME
Vegetable Gardening

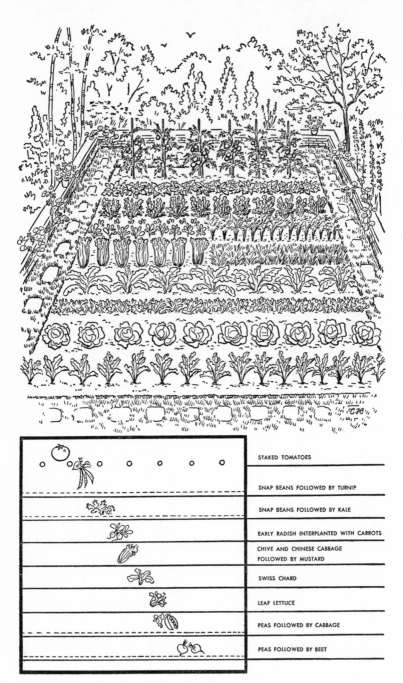

	STAKED TOMATOES
	SNAP BEANS FOLLOWED BY TURNIP
	SNAP BEANS FOLLOWED BY KALE
	EARLY RADISH INTERPLANTED WITH CARROTS
	CHIVE AND CHINESE CABBAGE FOLLOWED BY MUSTARD
	SWISS CHARD
	LEAF LETTUCE
	PEAS FOLLOWED BY CABBAGE
	PEAS FOLLOWED BY BEET

GARDEN PLAN 20′x 20′

CHAPTER I

Planning the Vegetable Garden

When we mean to build,
We first survey the plot, then draw the model.
KING HENRY IV II.i.3.

The first step toward a good garden is the making of a plan, and it is one of the most pleasant exercises of the gardener's year. It is begun well in advance of sowing time, so that supplies may be ordered, flats and frames prepared and sown, and the soil properly fitted; all in good time, so as to avoid that scramble which is the prelude to disappointment.

In warm Southern areas the autumn sun may be strong when preparations are made for cool-weather crops to be grown in winter, but spring, as its very name indicates, is the universal beginning of the season. It begins to stir within the gardener on the arrival of the new catalogs, and though a winter wind may be howling as he reads them, emulation surges in him before the sap rises in the trees.

Many considerations go into the planning of even a

3

small garden: the location, the soil, the climate, the preferences of the household, the gardener's ambition— and the degree of his forgetfulness of the hoe. Therefore it is no more to be expected than it is to be desired that there will be any uniformity in garden plans, and those which follow here are intended only as suggestions from the criticism of which the gardener may evolve his own arrangement.

The vegetable garden should be close to the kitchen door, and to make it as small as possible is a better aim than to make it as large as possible, with due regard, of course, to what is to be grown. There is often a temptation to lay out a larger area than the gardener can conveniently cultivate, but a small garden well worked may be quite as productive as a larger one that is just beyond the gardener's limitations. Certainly it will be far more pleasing to the eye—an aspect of vegetable gardening which is not to be neglected.

The plan should be so worked out as to make full use of whatever sized area is decided upon and to avoid the waste of land, money, time, and effort that are involved in growing more than is necessary of any item. By selecting carefully what is to be grown, by planting a little at a time rather than a whole row, and by using varieties of differing maturity, it should be the aim to provide continuous supplies throughout the growing season and into the winter, not a superfluity of something one week and nothing of anything the next week.

In deciding which vegetables to grow, it is well to remember that some give small return for the space they occupy but are usually plentiful at the stores; for example, cucumber, pumpkin, sweet potato, and watermelon, even potato for any but a large garden. Some are difficult to raise successfully, as celery, or not adapted to the soil and climate, as okra in the more northerly states or parsnip in the more southerly. On the other hand, some are seldom available at the stores yet are not difficult to grow, as chard, mustard, cress, dill, chive, and other herbs; or are far better in quality and flavor when fresh picked as peas, asparagus, corn, leaf lettuce, and endive. And, almost inevitably, if you want what is new or unusual you must grow it yourself, for the market gardener necessarily must cater to the general demand.

A useful rough guide in planning a succession to early vegetables is the old rule that root plants follow leaf plants and vice versa. This does not cover all species—corn or tomatoes, for example, which may follow almost any early crop.

THE SMALL VEGETABLE GARDEN

This little garden, though but twenty feet square, is arranged for a dozen vegetables by intercropping and succession, which will furnish good potherbs and simple salads throughout the season. If worked with care it will provide a small family with much of its vegetable supply, many a treat in flavor and quality, and many a bonus of

1   CORN MIDSEASON — INTERPLANTED WITH WINTER SQUASH OR POLE BEANS

    EARLY CORN

2   LIMA BEANS OR EDIBLE SOYBEANS

3   SUMMER SQUASH

4   STAKED TOMATOES

5   BEANS FOLLOWED BY KALE

    BEANS FOLLOWED BY TURNIP

6   CARROTS FOLLOWED BY CHINESE CABBAGE

7   PARSNIP WITH EARLY RADISH

8   LETTUCE

9   ONIONS: BULB AND SCALLION

10 EARLY BEETS FOLLOWED BY ESCAROLLE

11 WITLOOF CHICORY AND EGGPLANT

12 MUSTARD AND CHINESE CABBAGE FOLLOWED BY KOHLRABI

13 SWISS CHARD OR NEW ZEALAND SPINACH

14 SECOND PEAS FOLLOWED BY CABBAGE

15 EARLY PEAS FOLLOWED BY BROCCOLI

16 HERB BORDER

17 SEEDLINGS, CHIVE, SHALLOTS, ETC.

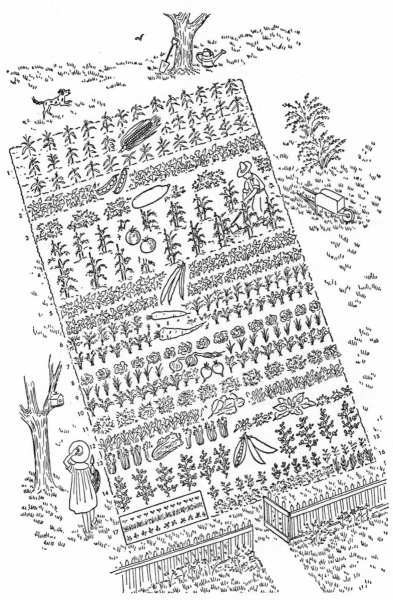

GARDEN PLAN 30'x 40'

vitamins. More may be grown in this area than is indicated on the plan, for the rows can be closer together if the soil is well prepared.

Corn takes too much space for such a small plot; tomatoes also need a lot of space but they yield better returns and are easy to raise. Some might deny the peas a place, for it cannot be claimed that, foot for foot, their poundage is high, but peas are only at their best when fresh picked, and their harvest is early enough to allow a later vegetable in the row. Leaf lettuce and Swiss chard are "cut-and-come-again" vegetables, worth their place in any garden. For the other rows there is a wide range of choice.

THE MEDIUM–SIZED GARDEN

For a family of four and occasional guests this garden will afford vitamins, salads, and vegetable dishes galore, with additional health-giving properties in its opportunity for exercise to a spare-time gardener and his household satellites.

It might almost be called a packet garden, since a packet of seed will serve to sow most of the rows, and it is so arranged for succession plantings that there will be no idle space throughout the growing season. Corn, as the tallest crop, is placed at the back; the salad vegetables and herbs toward the front, which is presumed to be nearer the kitchen.

Whether there is room for three rows of corn in a

garden of this size is for individual taste and judgment, but the space as shown is not wholly given over to this luxuriance; pole beans may climb the stalks or vining squash wind its way around them. In those parts of the South where sweet corn does not thrive, this area might be better occupied by okra, pole beans, and more tomatoes, and somewhere in such gardens a row of collard must find a place.

THE LARGE GARDEN

This is the plan, with slight modifications, of a Connecticut home garden grown in 1941. It is ample for a family of six or eight and would provide sufficient employment for half the week of a working gardener, though this one was successfully tended by the head of a household, a businessman who was enthusiastic enough to give all his spare time to it, aided by occasional help and efficient garden tools.

An objection that might be raised to this plan is that the rows are interrupted by paths, but neither horse nor tractor was used except in preliminary plowing and harrowing, and the rows are quite long enough for the one-man power behind a wheel hoe and its various attachments.

The rows run approximately north and south for benefit of sun; the perennial plants are back on one side, the tall corn on the other, and the centerpiece of the plan is a plot of herbs about eight feet in diameter with a pole

GARDEN PLAN 50' x 100'

as pivot. Not shown in the plan is the cold frame essential to a garden of this size, which was elsewhere in the lee of a sheltering wall.

Adjacent to the corn is a planting of bush Lima beans designed for succotash, and with them a trial of edible soybeans. The kale border, half Dwarf Green and half Variegated, is ornamental as well as useful, and is neatly offset by its kindred across the path.

The miscellaneous vegetables in the bottom left section are not likely to be the same, or at least similarly disposed, in any two gardens, but the grouping is sufficiently varied both in salad plants and potherbs. A succession row to the first planting of Chinese cabbage is not indicated because New Zealand spinach sprawls; the distance between these two rows is rather close so that there will be sprawling room when the Chinese cabbage is finished.

Obvious omissions from this plan are potatoes, cucumbers, and melons; the space is there had the gardener wished to grow them.

CHAPTER II

The Garden Soil

A gardener's first concern is with the soil, and some knowledge of its nature and functioning is fundamental to success in his work.

Time was when this upper crust of earth in which we dig was regarded as so much inanimate "matter." Today there are those who go to the other extreme, endowing it in their minds with mystic properties.

Between these opposing views is the knowledge gained by soil science which in relatively recent years has developed an understanding of a complex subject that is invaluable to agriculture.

What Is Soil?

The bulk of the soil is disintegrated rock of many kinds reduced to a fine granular state by the action of heat and frost, the oxygen and carbon dioxide of the air, glaciers, wind, lichens, and other causes. This inorganic material constitutes 65 per cent to 95 per cent of the whole. Organic matter, provided by plants and animals, alive and dead, forms 2 per cent to 5 per cent. Of the rest, part is soil air with less oxygen and more carbon dioxide than the atmosphere and part soil water holding in solution mineral salts from which plants derive materials necessary for their growth.

Here it may be noted that plants, by their unique ability to convert inorganic materials into organic, make existence possible for all other living creatures.

Soil Types

Clay soils usually contain 25 per cent to 30 per cent of clay, which may be described as most minutely ground rock, putty-like when damp but drying out solid as a brick. Such soils, when dug wet, will form clods that are very difficult to work. The surface may become very hard, with large cracks in it, while the soil below is cold and wet, since soil water exists as a film on individual particles, and the microscopic particles of clay are so innumerable that the proportion of water may be as high as 40 per cent. But clay soils are capable of great improvement by the addition of organic matter, which they usually lack, and then their tendency to retain moisture makes them very suitable for main and late crops. Lime is helpful, but as to sand there is an old saying which is still generally true:

> *Sand in clay is money thrown away,*
> *Clay in sand is money in hand.*

Silt soils are made up of somewhat coarser though still very minute particles and will not dry into such impervious solids as clay. They hold moisture well and, with the addition of organic matter, are very desirable as garden soils.

Sandy soils have a large proportion of particles big enough to be individually seen and felt, consequently they drain and dry out rather quickly. They also warm up early and for these reasons are more suitable for the first, quick-growing crops than for those of long season. They can, however, be built into the best of garden soils with manure and compost, the texture and moisture-holding qualities being thus greatly improved and plant nutrients retained instead of being leached away.

Loam is the term used to denote a medium soil with a fairly even proportion of clay, silt, and sand. If one or other of these predominates, the soil is a clay loam, silt loam, or sandy loam. Containing a due proportion of organic matter, loam is the ideal for gardening.

Peat and muck soils are composed chiefly of the remains of plants in bygone generations, therefore they contain but little inorganic matter. As they absorb and hold much water they are "late" soils—that is, their crops are late—but they are easy to work. Their nitrogen content, 1 per cent to 2 per cent, is high but they are low in minerals, especially potash. When improved they are exceptionally good for growing vegetables.

Topsoil is the upper fertile stratum, varying in depth

from a matter of inches to several feet. Beneath it lies the *subsoil,* lifeless and inorganic, though penetrated by the deep roots of many plants foraging for minerals and moisture.

ORGANIC CONTENT OF SOIL

Though it forms but a small proportion of the whole, the organic matter in soil is of the greatest importance by far, since its presence there is essential to plant life. Apart from the living and mostly microscopic flora and fauna with which a fertile loam is teeming, it consists of the remains of previous plant and animal life, either decomposed into humus or in process of being turned into that highly complex substance through the action of innumerable active creatures, from bacteria to earthworms. Bacteria, which form about 75 per cent of the soil flora, are plants of very simple, single-celled structure, multiplying themselves rapidly by splitting, and are so exceedingly minute that billions of them of different types may exist in a cubic inch of fertile soil.

Earthworms are plentiful in such soil and add to its fertility by passing great quantities of it, together with vegetative material and other organic matter, through their digestive processes, to the amount of as much as ten tons per acre in the course of a year, at the same time greatly improving the aeration and irrigation of the soil through their workings. Beetles, grubs, and other insects, burrowing animals, wind, and rain, also contribute to the moving and mixing of soil.

Humus

Humus is a term quite generally applied to even partly decomposed matter in the soil, though its more accurate meaning is organic matter so far decayed that it has lost its original identity. Its composition has not been determined yet, because of difficulty in extracting the humic material from the mineral elements of the soil with which it is associated, but it is the end product of those myriad soil microorganisms which effect decay. Of its value and action in the soil, however, there is no doubt. It binds the mineral particles of sandy soils, thus retaining moisture and plant food; it lightens clay soils so that they are more readily drained; it contains plant foods in assimilable form; it provides a source of energy and suitable surroundings for essential soil organisms; it takes up and retains water, thus helping to give to the soil an evenly diffused moisture content. It also checks the effects of extremes in temperature.

Inorganic Content of Soil

Garden plants manufacture their principal food in the leaves, where carbon dioxide from the air and water taken up through the roots are combined to form sugar and starches or carbohydrates. But they also require from the soil a variety of elements, mostly in minute quantities.

For example: An analysis of a corn crop by means of sample plants showed that 70 per cent of the whole was water. When this had been dried out, the elements left were approximately in the following proportions:

Oxygen	44.57%	
Carbon	43.70	
Hydrogen	6.26	
	———	94.53%
Nitrogen	1.46	
Silicon	1.17	
Potassium	.92	
Calcium	.23	
Phosphorus	.20	
Magnesium	.18	
Sulphur	.17	
Chlorine	.14	
Aluminum	.11	
Iron	.08	
Manganese	.03	
Sodium and other elements unde-termined	.78	
	———	5.47%

Other crops would of course show different analyses but this will suffice to illustrate the wide range of inorganic elements supplied by the soil, all of which, however small in quantity, are necessary for the health and balanced growth of the plant. Thus the magnesium in the example above, amounting to less than three ounces in one hundred pounds, is important out of all proportion to its quantity. Its absence would have resulted in stunted, yellow-leaved plants, since magnesium is a component part of chlorophyll, which not only colors leaves green but is the heart of their food manufacturing operations.

How Inorganic Food Is Formed

A small part of these elements and their compounds is added to the soil from the dust and gases of the atmosphere, largely washed down by rain, but they are chiefly derived from the disintegration of rocks and the decay of organic material, much of which results, as a by-product, from the growth and activity of microorganisms. Organic acids developed in the processes of decay have an important part, through their action on mineral fractions of the soil, in the series of changes which result in compounds that can be assimilated by plants.

Nitrifying Bacteria

Though nitrogen forms about 80 per cent of the air it cannot—or very rarely, if at all—be used in the gaseous form by garden plants which, with the exception of legumes, derive their supplies of this vital element chiefly from nitrates produced through a series of operations by at least four different species of bacteria. Ammonia, formed at one stage of the series, is also a source.

The legumes, which include peas, beans, clovers, lupines, and other species, are infested with certain bacteria living in their roots, where they give rise to characteristic nodules or swellings. These bacteria take nitrogen gas from the air and build it into proteins, thus providing the plant with supplies of nitrogen within its irritated roots. When the plant dies much of the nitrogenous material is added to the soil as its roots decay—a reason for growing and plowing-under legumes to enrich soil.

Denitrifying Bacteria

The effects of soil bacteria are not invariably beneficial to the inorganic food supply. One type which, unlike others in the soil, does not require oxygen and flourishes in poorly drained or waterlogged soils, breaks down nitrates, releasing their nitrogen to the air.

Replenishing the Soil

In the seasonal cycle of growth and decay, plants usually fall to earth where they stood, and thus a relatively stable balance of the soil constituents is naturally maintained. But when plants are continually removed, the soil becomes more and more impoverished; what was built up in the slow annual processes of many centuries may in a few years be quite depleted. Fertility can be restored only by the addition of materials providing those elements in which the soil has become deficient, and for this purpose the gardener uses farmyard manure, compost, catch crops, lime, and commercial fertilizers.

CHAPTER III

Fertilizers

MANURE

Well-rotted manure is generally ranked first as a means of compensating the soil for the nutrient elements taken from it by cropping. For most suburban gardeners, however, and even for many in rural areas, this by-product of the farm is out of reach by reason of its scarcity or its cost, so the compost heap and cover crops are becoming increasingly popular as the sources of supplies for humus materials.

Where manure is available it usually contains a large amount of straw from the animals' bedding, and both must be well decomposed before use in the garden, except when it is to be dug in during fall cleaning up and fitting operations. New manure of whatever kind—horse, cow, and especially poultry—should therefore be composted by mixing it with soil, preferably under a roof, keeping the heap damp but not so wet that soluble materials may be leached out, and turning it over with a fork every six or eight weeks. A layer of soil on top of the pile prevents loss of ammonia.

Professional gardeners make an excellent compost by building alternate layers of manure, soil, and sod or leaf mold.

Livestock manure varies in its constituents, depending on the animals from which it came and the feed they consumed, but only small amounts of nitrogen and potassium are lost in passage through the digestive tracts. Where legumes have been fed, more nitrogen may be returned to the field than was taken from it by the growing plants. Phosphates enter largely into the composition of bones and milk, therefore manure is apt to be lacking in this item and superphosphate or bone meal may be added to the garden soil to replace it.

How Much Manure?

The amount of manure required for the garden will be determined more by its availability and its cost than by any consideration of how much the soil requires. It is highly improbable that too much, if the manure is old, will be added. Two tons spread evenly over a 50 × 100 ft. garden would mean a pound and a quarter per square foot; as manure is 75 per cent water, the addition of organic matter would be four ounces. This would be a rich application; and for such a garden one ton supplemented by commercial fertilizer would probably be more satisfactory from every point of view.

The soil will then be enriched in every way—in humus material and attendant bacteria, in mineral constituents, and in all the vitamin B and hormone-encouraging chemicals that any growing plant may need.

Synthetic Manure

During World War I scarcity of manure and intensity of vegetable production in England led to a study at Rothamsted Experimental Station, the premier institution of its kind, from which resulted a process and a chemical formula on which a patent was issued. The material used was chiefly straw, but work done at various American experiment stations has shown that even cornstalks, with other garden refuse, may be added. At the Michigan Station a ton of dry straw was satisfactorily treated with a mixture of sixty pounds of ammonium sulphate (20 per cent nitrogen), twenty pounds of superphosphate (20 per cent phosphoric acid), and sixty pounds of finely ground limestone. A layer of the material to be treated is made about a foot thick, well tramped down and watered, then sprinkled with the fertilizer salts; then another layer, tramped, watered, and sprinkled; and so on until the heap is about five feet high, when it is finished with a concave top so that it will hold rain or other water, which must be added as frequently as is necessary to keep the material damp. Fermentation soon begins, and in a few months of warm weather will produce a very good substitute for rotted farmyard manure, about three times the original volume due to the added water and the effects of fermentation.

COMPOST

No well-regulated garden is complete without its compost heap, which not only provides an excellent and inexpensive source of humus and soil regeneration but also promotes tidiness, thus enhancing the appearance of the area and adding to the pleasure of the gardener so that more and better gardening results.

Commercial fertilizers do not add humus to the soil, except indirectly through the production of extra roots which remain in place, and their continued use without the addition of organic matter may eventually result in a soil that is caked and tired.

The site for the compost heap should be in a shaded place, and there a shallow pit is dug, five or six feet wide, a foot or more deep, and as long as seems necessary. The soil dug out will be used to cover the heap. First throw in a layer of old cornstalks, sunflower stalks, or the like heavy trash—but not wood or branches—smashing them up as well as possible. On this spread manure about three inches deep if it is available; if not, use good topsoil and humus instead. Dust this liberally with a complete commercial fertilizer, then add a layer of six to twelve inches of leaves, lawn clippings, vegetable refuse from the kitchen, weeds—provided they do not carry seeds—in fact, almost anything that will decay, except plants infested with disease or insect pests, which should be burned. As the material is gradually added, a little ground limestone may be shaken among it. When this layer is thick enough, dust it also with fertilizer and spread over it three or four inches of topsoil with some old compost or manure if there is any.

Build such alternating layers until the pile is four or five feet high, and see that it is kept moist. Top it off with a light layer of soil, lower in the center than at the sides so as to hold water. As the heap is built it should slope slightly in from the base, and soil may be added to the sloping sides three or four inches thick. In most gardens there is not enough material around to build up to five feet at the outset; layers are added as occasion arises, and when the heap is topped the pit is lengthened and a new section begun.

If started in the spring, forked over once or twice to mix it thoroughly, and prevented from drying, there will be humus by fall; dark, friable, clean, devoid of any smell but that of rich earth and so perfect for the garden that there need be no fear of ever adding too much. When dug out, it should be sliced vertically, going clear down to the bottom of the heap rather than working horizontally along the top. Any woody pieces or tough stalks not fully decayed should be thrown to the other end of the pile on the new section there.

The relatively small amount of work involved in gradually building a compost heap is out of all proportion to the dividends it pays, and once the gardener has acquired a sense of humus he will look with horror on such benighted pagans as that modern poet who prays, as he pokes his unhallowed bonfire,

God of gardeners, accept this coil
Of acrid smoke . . .

Liquid Manure

Liquid manure is a powerful stimulant for plants and an enriching solution to use in wetting the compost heap. In this form, a little manure goes a long way, for what would be very slowly soaked out of manure in the ground by rain is here made available in a strong dose. Only old manure should be used, and at the rate of a half bushel to fifty gallons of water. On this basis put into an old gunny sack as much (or rather as little, because the tendency is to make the stuff too strong) as is required for whatever barrel or tub you fill with water. Let it stand for a few days, but stir it occasionally; the spent manure can then be thrown on the compost heap and the liquid lightly poured adjacent to but not on the vegetables that may be in need of dynamic treatment.

COMMERCIAL FERTILIZERS

Any material which makes the soil more fertile is a fertilizer. Chemical compounds intended for this purpose and supplied through the channels of trade and commerce are commercial fertilizers, or artificial fertilizers, as distinct from manure, which comes from the farm and is a natural by-product.

The principal elements supplied by commercial fertilizers are the three that plants chiefly require from the soil: nitrogen, phosphorus, and potash, which have been compared, very roughly, to proteins, fats, and vitamins in human nutrition. All three are present in what is known as a *complete* fertilizer (though small quantities of many others would be needed to make it truly complete), and when the amounts of each of the three are in that ratio to one another which best suits particular plant growth, it is a *balanced* fertilizer.

NITROGEN

Nitrogen is the leaf maker and of vital importance in the whole vegetative development of plants. High nitrogen content helps the leafy species, but if present in excess may have an adverse effect on species cultivated for their seed or fruits, since blossoming is apt to be retarded while stems and leaves are overdeveloped. Conversely, nitrogen deficiency is seen in stunted plants with yellow leaves.

While nitrogen is the most important of the three main constituents of commercial fertilizers, it is at the same time the most likely to be needed, since nitrates are readily taken up by plants and also are easily leached away from soil.

It is calculated that the air above a single acre of

ground includes 35,000 tons of nitrogen, but as plants are not adapted to take their essential supplies of this element in gaseous form they largely depend, in the natural cycle, upon the activities of nitrogen-fixing bacteria, and the small amount, averaging five pounds per acre per annum, of nitrates and ammonia formed in the soil by chemical reactions with the nitrogen washed down by rain from this inexhaustible atmospheric supply.

Nitrate of soda, which is used as a top-dressing for growing plants, is the quickest way of supplying nitrogen but the least lasting in the soil because it is very soluble. It tends to produce an alkaline reaction through its sodium residue. Sulphate of ammonia is less soluble but is likely to increase acidity by leaving sulphuric acid after its nitrogen has been absorbed. These must be used with care as they are harmful in overdoses and they must not be allowed to come into direct contact with plants. Bone meal, which is used primarily for its high phosphorus content, also contains from 1 per cent to 3 per cent nitrogen. It is a slow-acting fertilizer but safe, as it cannot damage the plants.

Phosphorus

Phosphorus is necessary for the process of cell division by which plants grow. It is the ripener and fortifier, important in root development, resistance to disease, and in maturing fruits and seeds. When it is lacking, plants are subnormal and dwarfed, the leaves are usually very deep green, often with a yellow margin, and fall early; if seeds are formed they are likely to be small and shriveled.

Phosphorus also has accessory effects: in the soil its presence is necessary to certain nitrogen-fixing bacteria (Azotobacter), while in plants it tends to correct the effects of overstimulation from too much nitrogen.

Although it is such an important element of plant and animal life, being part of every living cell, pure phosphorus is never found in nature; it exists in compounds such as phosphates, which are salts of phosphoric acid, particularly tricalcium phosphate, the important constituent of bones and phosphate rock.

Superphosphate, or acid phosphate, is produced by treating phosphate rock with sulphuric acid to render it more soluble and is one of the most valuable commercial fertilizers.

Bone meal, formerly a very popular garden fertilizer but not now so generally used, contains about 25 per cent phosphorus but is so slow-acting that little of this is available until the season after application, even if the bones have been very finely ground. An overdose of it, however, will not burn plants as would some of the inorganic fertilizers, and it is of good service for indoor plants or top dressing.

POTASSIUM

The third element in the fertilizer trio is more frequently referred to as potash, which is one of its oxides, a compound which takes its name from an old process of manufacturing it by mixing wood ashes with water and evaporating the liquor from an iron pot. The process is obsolete, but wood ashes still contain from 4 per cent to 8 per cent of potash and should always be saved to scatter on the garden. Hardwood ashes have the highest content, coal ashes have none and are useless, or worse, in the garden except on paths.

Natural deposits of potassium salts now form the source of supply for commercial fertilizers. Muriate of potash, a trade name for potassium chloride, is used when it is necessary to supply this element separately and not as a complete fertilizer, as in sandy and muck soils. Potassium sulphate is sometimes recommended but is more expensive and little, if any, more effective. For the average garden, however, there is plenty of potash in manure or compost, and complete fertilizers always include it.

Potash is a stem and structure builder, essential to the formation of carbohydrates, and therefore of particular value to root crops such as carrots, parsnips, turnips, etc., as well as to the stem plants—celery and rhubarb. Its deficiency in the soil will be shown by weak plants, usually with yellowish-brown mottling of the leaves, which break down.

ANALYSIS

A bag of complete fertilizer bears, by law, an analysis of the contents in the form of three numbers; for example, 5-10-5, indicating the percentages of nitrogen, phosphoric acid (more accurately phosphorus pentoxide, which is phosphoric acid minus water), and potash. The nutrient salts are always named in that order and the figures are always percentages; the rest of the material in the bag is filler, that is, inert matter such as sand. This filler is not a mere waste, for without it the chemicals would be in too strong concentration for use. The present tendency, however, is toward higher concentrations than were used in the past, and some states insist on not less than 20 per cent total. Thus 4-8-4, which has been extensively used as a general-purpose fertilizer, might be replaced by 8-16-8 if it were desired to maintain precisely the same ratio (see *ratio*, below). Very highly concentrated fertilizers are not too desirable because of the difficulty of dispersing them evenly and widely through the soil, and because low-analysis fertilizers usually contain, as impurities, some of the minor elements that may be of value. The cost per bag, of course, increases with the concentration.

FORMULA

The formula of a fertilizer goes further than the analysis and shows the materials used. Keeping the same example of 5-10-5 we might have:

2½ per cent nitrogen as 15 per cent sodium nitrate
2½ per cent nitrogen as 20 per cent ammonium sulphate
10 per cent phosphoric acid as 20 per cent superphosphate
5 per cent potash as 48 per cent potassium chloride

This means that 2½ per cent of the contents of the bag is nitrogen in the form of a product which by itself contains 15 per cent sodium nitrate, and so on. The importance of this information lies in the fact that some compounds are more soluble, therefore quicker acting, than others; and that some affect the acidity or alkalinity of the soil more than others.

RATIO

Fertilizer ratio is a term sometimes used in discussions of soil treatment. It merely expresses the proportions of the three elements, as 1-2-1 (instead of 5-10-5) to show that there is twice as much phosphoric acid as nitrogen, and the same proportion of nitrogen as of potash. In short, the ratio is qualitative rather than quantitative.

LIME

Lime is usually classed as a soil amendment but, apart from the fact that calcium, of which it largely consists, is a nutrient, it is a fertilizer within our definition of that term, since many plants are benefited by its application to the soil. Its function is not only to reduce acidity: it improves the texture of clay soils by making them more friable, or crumbly, and of sandy soils by making them more compact; it nullifies the toxic effects of some undesirable soil compounds such as those of aluminum and iron; it forms other chemical combinations in the soil which result in making more nitrogen, phosphorus, and potash available as plant food; and it creates conditions more favorable for beneficial microorganisms, especially those which cause decomposition.

Soil Acidity

The principal function of lime, however, is the reduction of acidity—a condition which may be caused in the soil by the loss of calcium and other non-acid substances, largely through leaching by soil water and consumption by plants. This leaves in the soil the acid compounds which are formed in processes of organic decay and their action on the minerals. Thus the mineral nature of the soil and its underlying rocks have a determining effect on acidity and its opposite, alkalinity.

Testing for Acidity

The rough-and-ready method of testing for acidity or alkalinity is by placing a strip of litmus paper in a handful of moist soil. Blue litmus turns red in acid soil, red litmus turns blue in alkaline, both turn purple if the soil is neutral. This gives but little indication of the amount of correction required, which may be better gauged by inexpensive soil-testing kits or learned with accuracy by sending a sample to the nearest agricultural experiment station.

*p*H

The *p*H scale (*p* for parts, H for hydrogen ion concentration)* is used to measure the active, though not

*Technically it is the logarithm of the reciprocal of the gram

the total, acidity or alkalinity. This scale is graduated from 1 to 14, the middle or neutral point, as in purified distilled water, being 7. Numbers below 7 indicate acidity; above 7, alkalinity. Vinegar has a pH value of 3, from the acetic acid it contains; and ammonia, a strong alkali, registers pH 11; but though such ordinary substances may be near one or other end of the scale, a range of pH 4.5 to pH 8 covers all the reactions of cultivable soils, thus

pH	Soil Reaction	pH	Soil Reaction
4.5	Very acid	7.0	Neutral
5.0	Acid	7.25	Slightly alkaline
5.5	Medium acid	7.5	Medium alkaline
6.0	Slightly acid	7.75	Strongly alkaline
6.5	Very slightly acid	8.0	Very strongly alkaline

It will be noticed that there are 2.5 units on the acid side and only one unit on the alkaline side, within the limits of plant growth. The scale being logarithmic, each unit on it represents a tenfold change in acidity or alkalinity. Thus compared with a soil of pH 6, one of pH 5 is ten times as acid and one of pH 4 is a hundred times as acid.

Most garden vegetables thrive better in a soil that is slightly acid, where plant food is likely to be better bal-

ionic hydrogen equivalent per liter; in water the equivalents of H and OH ions are each 10^{-7}; pH 7 therefore represents neutrality.

anced than in alkaline or even neutral soils. Few can tolerate sour alkaline soils, and undue acidity may be accompanied by toxic compounds of aluminum, iron, etc.

So many factors condition the growth of a plant that it is not practicable to attempt any more than a rough classification as to their soil *p*H preferences. Such is the following, issued by the Connecticut Experiment Station:

*p*H 5.0 to 5.6	*p*H 5.2 to 6.0	*p*H 5.6 to 6.8	*p*H 6.0 to 7.2
Potato	Eggplant	Beans	Beet
Sweet Potato	Pepper	Carrots	Broccoli
Watermelon	Tomato	Corn	Cabbage
		Parsley	Cucumber
		Parsnip	Endive

*p*H 5.6 to 6.8	*p*H 6.0 to 7.2	*p*H 6.4 to 7.6
Pumpkin	Leaf Lettuce	Asparagus
Salsify	Muskmelon	Cauliflower
Swiss Chard	Peas	Celery
Turnip	Radish	Leek
	Rhubarb	Head Lettuce
		Onion
		Spinach

To Correct Acidity

Various forms of lime are used for the correction of soil acidity: ground limestone (calcium carbonate), burned lime or quicklime (calcium oxide), and slaked or hydrated lime (calcium hydroxide).

Ground limestone is the slowest-acting of the three

and best suited for fall application, when it is broadcast and worked into the top three or four inches of soil. Burned lime is inconvenient for the gardener because it is in awkward lumps and it must be slaked by adding water in a tub or a hole in the ground to make it less caustic, except when the lumps are scattered on unbroken land and left to be hydrated by air moisture and rain.

Hydrated lime is a powder, easy to distribute and quick-acting. The rate of application necessary in particular cases will be indicated by a soil test, but in general it may be dusted at the rate of two hundred pounds over a plot of 50 × 100 ft. or fifty pounds if the plot is 25 × 50 ft., and raked in well.

Lime should never be applied at the same time as manure or fertilizer. Preferably ground limestone in the fall should precede fertilizer in the spring, but if a plot is being hurriedly conditioned and is known to need lime, let the fertilizer be dug in at least a week before liming and let another week elapse before planting.

To Correct Alkalinity

It is rarely necessary to make a garden soil more acid except in a limestone area or where continued watering with very hard water has led to an accumulation of alkaline salts. Correction to the extent of one pH unit, say from pH 7.5 to pH 6.5, may be expected from the application of aluminum sulphate—an inexpensive chemical—at the rate of one pound per square yard on medium loam soil; less on sandy soils, more on clay. This is to be worked into the soil and well though slowly watered. It it wise to make sure by test that the soil needs such strong medicine before administering it.

COVER CROPS: GREEN MANURE

Growing a temporary crop to be turned under for soil improvement is one of the most ancient farming practices. More than two thousand years ago the Chinese plowed in grass and weeds; the Greeks and Romans had found the virtue of legumes.

Following early vegetables or toward the harvest of others, a soil-improving crop may be planted not only to add the most inexpensive humus to the soil when it is turned under but also to prevent erosion; to prevent plant food from being leached away, by taking this up and holding it in the structures of the soil-improving plants to be returned later; to bring up plant food from the subsoil through its deep roots; and, if it be a legume, to add nitrogen to the soil.

Of the legumes, crimson clover may be sown among vegetable rows after midsummer, or red clover, which is winter-hardy, in the more northerly areas. Lespedeza is extensively used in the South for summer growth, bur clover for winter. A pound of seed will go a long way in even a large garden. Cowpeas are of great value on Southern soils where they are usually sown after spring vegetables have been harvested and before fall plantings.

Of the nonlegumes, rye is the most generally suitable as it grows freely on practically any soil and may be sown early or late. Buckwheat is very useful as a fast-growing summer crop but must be turned under before flowering, and better at 8″–10″ high. It is particularly valuable on land newly cleared for a garden. A peck (fourteen pounds) of rye or buckwheat seed will be ample for all the cover needed in a 50 × 100 ft. garden.

Green manure should be turned under while still tender and succulent and as far in advance of the succeeding planting as is practicable, so that its decomposition may be at least partial. As nonlegumes are being turned under they may advantageously be well sprinkled with sulphate of ammonia or other fertilizer high in nitrogen, to provide supplies of this element for the bacteria of decay and prevent their competing for it with the next crop to be planted.

Such competition is one reason why crops often do badly after coarse material such as cornstalks, woody stems, or straw has been plowed in. The soil bacteria increase greatly in number, using up much of the available nitrogen and producing a temporary deficiency of this vital element even though they ultimately return most of it to the soil.

MINOR ELEMENTS

In such a highly complex body as garden soil, there are many other substances than those mentioned above, many chemical reactions, many physical processes, but they are rather the concern of the soil scientist than the practical gardener. Some elements are necessary in measurable quantities, as calcium, sulphur, and magnesium; others in mere traces, such as boron, iron, manganese, and zinc. The minute quantities required are present in most soils and are usually replenished by constituents or impurities in commercial fertilizers.

PLANT SUPERCHARGERS

Nor need the cultivator concern himself with hormones, vitamins, and other bottles of proprietary preparations. He is better without them lest he be led to expect greater miracles than the sufficiently great one of natural growth; and as for his plants, they will find or make all the chemicals they need if he but give them good soil and proper surroundings.

CHAPTER IV

The Gardener's Tools

A gardener spends so much of his time with the tools of his trade that for him they come to acquire a familiarity which is not far from friendship, if they are good and helpful tools. Therefore, they should not be selected without some thought for their quality and for their suitability to the gardener's individual needs and preferences.

A small plot may be cultivated with a fork, a hoe, and a trowel; a large garden may require power equipment and an extensive range of accessories; in either case there is considerable variety in designs and materials, the value of which is not always to be measured in money. Good tools embody the results of a vast amount of experience and are designed for efficiency; cheap tools are usually made to sell at a price and are about as useful to the gardener as a cheap chisel to a carpenter. And the difference in initial cost is never very great, especially in view of the years of usage that are presumed to lie ahead.

Points to look for are efficiency in design for a particular purpose; quality and finish of the materials, especially steel; the heft, or weight and balance to suit the gardener's personal need; the extent of the garden and depth of the purse.

Spades are made in different sizes, weights, and shapes. For heavy soils a strong one, though not necessarily heavy, is advisable, but for lighter soils and average home gardens the so-called ladies' size, with smaller blade and shorter handle, will be found easy to use and quite efficient. The steel socket should extend well up the shaft, and the D grip should fit the hand comfortably.

A fork is the most useful of tools around the garden and may be had in different types designed to suit various soils and purposes. A digging fork has strong tines, sometimes square in section for heavy soils as in the English type, more usually of triangular section with the flat side uppermost; a manure fork has longer, more curved tines, circular in section; for lifting such crops as potatoes or beets there is a fork with many and lighter ball-pointed tines.

The hoe is almost synonymous with garden cultivation and, except for small plots, more than one will be worth having. The regular garden hoe is made with blades of differing width, depth, and weight; the Warren hoe blade is approximately heart-shaped, its pointed tip used in opening drills and inverted to close the drills; the

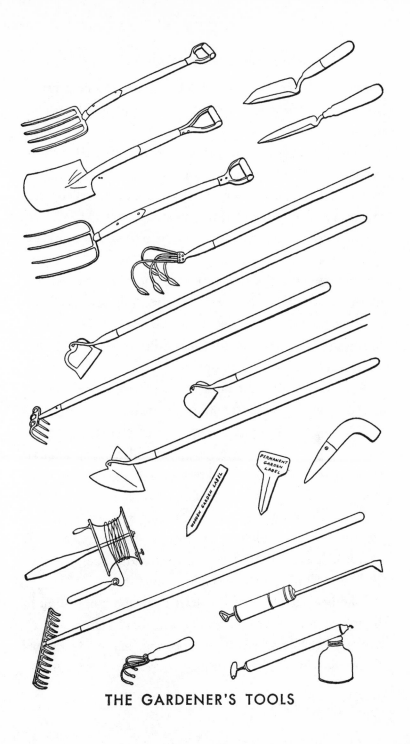

THE GARDENER'S TOOLS

scuffle or D-hoe has a flat blade adapted to cut weeds below the surface; and several other types will be found in the tool catalogs.

Before buying any hoe, it is well to examine the various types and sizes that are available; do not choose one that is heavier than is necessary, and test its balance to make sure that it is suited to its user as well as to its use.

MAXIM: *Time spent sharpening a hoe is time well spent.*

A trowel is not just a trowel: a good one, forged out of the solid, correctly tempered and well balanced, is a pleasure to handle; a cheap one with a soft nose and a loose grip is an abomination. In addition to the standard garden type, a narrow transplanting trowel is very useful.

A rake is useful not only in keeping the garden tidy but in finishing and smoothing seedbeds. Its steel head may be of the D or bow type, or of the level, direct-socket type; in either the socket should be long enough to be well fitted and pinned to the shaft so that they may not work loose or even part company later on.

For general cultivation and stirring the upper soil to form a surface mulch, a hand cultivator is useful. It is more or less a cross between a fork and a hoe, and may be had with fixed or adjustable prongs.

The heavier work of the garden can be immeasurably lightened and expedited by the wheel cultivator with its various attachments for performing many operations from plowing before planting to raking after harvest.

The single-wheel type is convenient for the medium-sized garden and is capable of considerable adjustment to suit individual needs.

A wheelbarrow is almost essential in any garden of more than small to medium size where materials can be carried in bushel baskets, a supply of which should be in every garden large or small. For watering, overhead irrigation is essential to many commercial gardens but equipment de luxe to most others, where the hose and watering can are sufficient. Any hose of more than twenty-five feet should be provided with a reel.

A dibber, or dibble, is a short, stout, pointed stick used to make holes when transplanting. It should not be sunk so deep as to leave an air pocket below a plant. This precaution cannot be overemphasized.

Two stakes and a length of clothesline enable the gardener to mark his rows straight and symmetrically; when the rows are sown he may wish to identify them with labels which are usually pieces of wooden lath, though metal holders in which cards are inserted have the advantage of showing the name horizontally and last for years.

As the season progresses and insect pests appear, a duster or sprayer will probably be required. The type and size will depend upon the work to be done. Other convenient and useful pieces of equipment are to be found in the stores and the catalogs: as the fertilizer spreader, a miniature truck which assures even and measured distribution; the sieve or riddle to sift soil, compost, etc., the hand weeder, sickle, shears, whetstone, and on down to the refinement of kneeling pads.

The collection is not likely to be built up in a season or two; it begins with essentials, but later its extent is an indication of the endurance as well as the strength of the gardener's enthusiasm—tempered, of course, by his budget.

CARE OF THE TOOLS

If you may know a man by the company he keeps, you may equally know a gardener by the way he keeps his tools. After work, whatever tools have been in use should be scraped and rubbed with an oily rag of burlap, then hung on their own nail or put in their own place in the tool rack—a great aid to tidiness which can be easily made and screwed to the wall of the tool shed or garage. Failing a rack, there should be a shelf for the small tools and pegs or nails for those with D grips; the straight-shafted sort may be stood in a corner.

This tidiness with tools is no mere mental discipline; it is an insurance against losing one or leaving it out all night, for its absence from the rack will be as obvious as a missing tooth; it saves time and temper when a wanted tool can at once be had; and sharp, clean tools are always more efficient than those caked with dirt or blunted and rusty.

If tools are well cleaned and greased before being laid aside for the winter they are likely to be fit for use in spring, but when, through inadvertence, or through coming into possession of old tools somewhere, it is necessary to remove rust, a soaking in kerosene will be helpful, or for stubborn cases a paste may be made of one part glycerine, two parts phosphoric acid, and five parts ground silica. The paste is to be applied to the rusted surface, allowed to stand in a warm place for twenty to thirty minutes, then washed off.

CHAPTER V

Raising Seedlings

FLATS

It is often desirable, and in some cases it is necessary, to sow seeds under cover and later transfer the young plants to their place in the garden. Thus an early start is given to species that require a long period for maturity, that flourish better in cool weather, or that are unfitted to endure cold. Whatever the crop, it is a satisfaction to see it growing strongly, with promise of harvest enhanced.

Seeds are accordingly often sown in shallow boxes known as flats some weeks in advance of the time for transplanting. Any clean box, including a cigar box, may be used, but standard flats of cypress or redwood, which endure the damp conditions of use, may be bought either as boards ready to be nailed together or already assembled. Sizes vary, but 12″ × 18″ × 3″ is convenient, and 16″ × 22″ × 3″ is largely used for flats in cold frames made of standard 3 ft. × 6 ft. sash.

The advantage of such flats for cold-frame work is that they can be lifted out and placed on a bench, which is a much easier level for the gardener than the ground.

Paper flats have recently been introduced: a longer outer box contains three or four long, narrow trays, each suitable for a single row when filled, pierced with small holes for water which is poured into the outer box.

Flats must have good drainage and therefore the bottom boards are left slightly apart, or holes are bored. A mixture is made of one part peat moss, one part sand, and one part finely sifted soil. The holes in the flat are covered with broken pieces of flowerpot or something of the sort, to retain soil but permit drainage; then the flat is filled with soil mixture and gently tamped down. Another method is to place a layer of coarse peat moss in the bottom of the flat, then soil, or soil and sand, finished on top with a very light layer of sterile sand or peat moss.

DAMPING-OFF

The purpose of this sterile top layer is to prevent damping-off—the death of the seedlings caused by various fungi which attack them at the surface or just below it and rot the stems, so that healthy-looking little plants often suddenly wilt and collapse. Some are so quickly attacked that they do not emerge from the soil; in either case there is no cure: prevention is the only safeguard, and to secure this several methods are used.

Keeping the surface of the soil reasonably dry is a de-

terrent to the growth of the fungi and therefore a flat
should be watered from below, not from above. It may
be set occasionally in an inch of water in a larger pan, or
it may be fitted with a wick reaching from the soil,
through a hole in the bottom board, to a dish of water
set between two pieces of 2″ × 2″ wood, on which the
flat will rest.

The microscopic organisms which cause damping-off
live for the most part in the soil, but they may be transmitted on seed. For this reason disinfectants are applied
sometimes to the soil, sometimes to the seed. Red copper
oxide, a dust which is obtainable at any seed store, is an
inexpensive and effective agent. For soil treatment, three
ounces in a gallon of water is the proportion, and enough
should be sprayed to give a thorough wetting as soon as
the seed has been sown in flat, frame, or hotbed. This is
to be repeated every week or ten days until the seedlings
are well established; the spray will not harm them and
it should get well in around their stems where the danger
may lie.

For seed treatment before sowing, the copper oxide
dust should be shaken vigorously with the seeds in a glass
jar, so that it is possible to see when they are coated, at
the rate of a teaspoonful to a pound of small seeds, or a
pinch to a packet. On large seeds such as pea, squash, or
cucumber, the dust will go five or six times as far.

Spergon is a highly efficacious new seed-treatment dust
which is devoid of poisonous metallic compounds.

Seeds of beans and all members of the cabbage tribe, including cabbage, cauliflower, broccoli, radish, and turnip, are sensitive to copper, and for these it is better to use zinc oxide, known in the paint store as zinc white, at the same rates as above. This may also be lightly dusted over the surface of the flat with good effect. Certain reliable proprietary preparations based on mercury compounds are also available and are to be used as directed on the containers.

Sterilization of the soil by baking it in a hot oven is sometimes recommended. This will kill the fungi and, if any are present, those microscopic eelworms known as nematodes, which often infest greenhouse soils in the North and the winter-warm garden soils of the South. But at the same time all beneficial organic matter in the soil is destroyed, and the gardener runs the risk of wrath in the kitchen if he attempts to put flats of soil in the oven. It would perhaps be more practicable to bake enough soil for a top layer of an eighth to a quarter of an inch deep.

Formaldehyde, or formalin, is often used and will kill fungi but not nematodes. In the form of 6 per cent dust, which may be purchased as such or home made by mixing fifteen parts of liquid formaldehyde with eighty-five parts of charcoal, it may be applied at the rate of about six ounces to a cubic foot of soil, thoroughly mixed, and well watered after being put in the flats. These may be sown on the following day, though it is better to wait

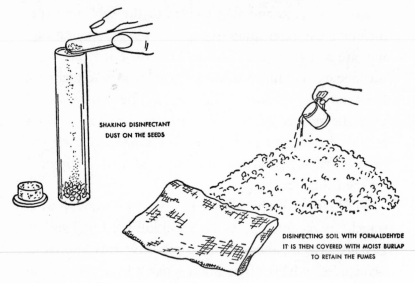

SHAKING DISINFECTANT
DUST ON THE SEEDS

DISINFECTING SOIL WITH FORMALDEHYDE
IT IS THEN COVERED WITH MOIST BURLAP
TO RETAIN THE FUMES

three or four days before using such treated soil for transplanting.

Liquid formaldehyde, which is of about 40 per cent concentration, may be applied at the rate of a small cupful to a gallon of water, soaking the soil, which should be covered with moist burlap or old papers for a couple of days to confine the fumes. Then it should be turned over daily for several days, until the disagreeable smell which attends liquid formaldehyde, though not the dust, has gone. The soil is thus well aerated and prevented from puddling. This treatment is extensively used in commercial nurseries. Formaldehyde fumes are toxic to vegetation and therefore must not be allowed near any seedlings. They are also irritating to the eyes and skin, so there should be good circulation of air where this disinfection is being done. Old flats and pots are apt to harbor the organisms of damping-off and should be well cleaned and disinfected before being used.

Sowing the Flat

The soil, which should be moist but not wet, is to be firmed down—not forgetting the corners and edges—with a block of wood and then marked in rows about two inches apart with any straightedge. The depth of sowing for large seeds is about twice their own diameter; the smaller seeds need be only barely covered, and to avoid their being crowded too thickly in the row are tapped gently from the packet, to which clean sand is sometimes added with a view to getting distribution of about five to ten seeds per inch. A small plant marker should be set at the end of the row for identification. The flat is then set in shallow water at room temperature so that it may be subirrigated, covered with a sheet of clean glass, paper, or burlap slightly raised to admit air. As seeds usually germinate better in darkness, the flat is kept covered until the seedlings appear, then gradually exposed to light.

Pricking out

Just after the first true leaves appear and the seedlings are from one to two inches high, they should be pricked out by lifting them gently with a pointed stick and setting in another flat or a frame, about two inches apart for all such plants as lettuce and the cabbage tribe; three to four inches apart for tomato, eggplant, and pepper. This gives them room to grow without becoming leggy and weak and enables the development of a strong root system necessary for successful transplanting to the open row in the garden. Bands, or bottomless cardboard boxes, are sometimes used at this stage for species which are difficult to transplant successfully when they have grown somewhat larger, as the bands can be set out in the garden later on without disturbing the roots.

SAND FLATS

A new method of raising seedlings is to use sand and chemical fertilizer instead of soil in the flat. The sand must be thoroughly washed to free it of all earth, then well drenched with boiling water to sterilize it; the flat too must be clean and sterilized. Some peat moss is placed in the bottom to aid drainage, next the damp sand, not quite filling up to the top of the flat, and then a sprinkling is given with a quart of water in which has been dissolved a teaspoonful of 5-10-5 or similar balanced fertilizer. The seeds are now sparsely sown and topped with clean, dry sand, after which the flat is covered as described above, to await germination. Obviously it must never be allowed to dry out, but when necessary should be stood in shallow water until enough has been taken up to make the surface moist. If the seedlings continue to make satisfactory growth, no more fertilizer is required,

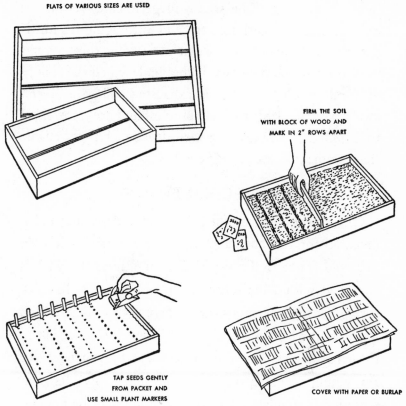

FLATS OF VARIOUS SIZES ARE USED

FIRM THE SOIL WITH BLOCK OF WOOD AND MARK IN 2″ ROWS APART

TAP SEEDS GENTLY FROM PACKET AND USE SMALL PLANT MARKERS

COVER WITH PAPER OR BURLAP

and in any event a teaspoonful to a quart of the sub-irrigation water once a week will be enough. This method avoids pricking out to another flat, though some thinning may be necessary, the seedlings remaining where they were sown until transplanted to the garden.

Alternatively the sand flat may be moistened with water only and no fertilizer added. In this case it is to be sown as in the usual sand flat, since the seedlings are to be pricked out later. The seed will germinate—fertility is not necessary for germination—and in foraging for nutrients the little plantlets will put out strong root systems until they are perhaps two inches high, when the supply of food within the seed is exhausted. They are then safely past the danger of damping off and are transferred to a soil flat, where their well-developed roots enable them to make speedy progress.

THE COLD FRAME

One of the most useful garden accessories and indispensable for full efficiency is the low structure known as a cold frame to distinguish it from a hotbed, which is equipped with some source of additional heat. In early spring it forms an intermediate stage for seedlings begun in the hotbed or indoors, prior to their being set out in the garden; in summer it provides a suitable starting place for young plants destined for autumn crops. Its construction is simple, and all the materials may be bought, if desired, in standard sizes ready for assembly. The location should be on the south side and the high end of the frame should back up to a wall, hedge, or bank that will shield it from the north wind.

The size of the frame will largely depend upon the extent of the garden but is usually in multiples of 6 × 3 ft., which is the standard size of the sash or window top, though smaller sashes of 4 × 2 ft. are also available and are very convenient, providing an adaptable unit which weighs only a third as much as the fifty pounds of the larger size. Glass substitutes of transparent plastic material reinforced with wire screen may be used in the sashes; they are lighter in weight than glass, though not so transparent, and have the great advantage of not being brittle. They deteriorate with time, however.

The walls of the frame should preferably be of cypress, redwood, or chestnut, not less than an inch thick, usually an inch and a half or even two inches, in lengths to suit the sash they support and carefully squared at the corners to make a correct rectangle. They are sunk six inches below ground level and supported at the corners on bricks. The hole to receive the frame, however, should be dug a foot deep and filled for four inches with gravel and coarse cinders to provide good drainage, then four inches of fine topsoil, with a top layer of rich soil, sand, and compost in equal parts. The construction can be done by any handy man, and the cost of the sash and

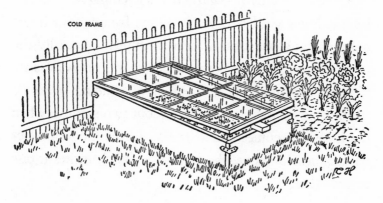

COLD FRAME

lumber will prove an investment returning high dividends over many years.

In use, the frame should be ventilated daily by raising the sash to whatever height is consistent with the temperature, the wind, and the progress of the young plants. If the nights are cold, the sash may be covered with a shutter or mat or both. Watering is to be done with discretion, for the soil should neither be flooded nor allowed to dry out; a fine spray is best and it should be given in the morning when necessary, so that the plants will not be wet at nightfall.

In summer the sash may be stored away and replaced by a lath screen, or one made of a light frame covered with old window screen, burlap, or other material to protect the young plants from extreme sunshine and heavy rain.

THE HOTBED

A hotbed is usually regarded as something of a luxury for the home gardener, yet it differs from a cold frame only in that some form of heat is supplied. Actually the same frame can serve both purposes, and often does so. If stable manure with its content of bedding straw be the heating agent, its effect lasts about two months, when the hotbed becomes a cold frame. In the modern, electrically heated frame, the turn of a switch makes it one or the other.

HOTBED: OLD STYLE

For the traditional hotbed, about four cubic yards of manure will be required for each standard sash, and it must be fresh. This should be kept under a roof if possible, moderately wetted, and allowed to stand for a week or so until arising steam shows active fermentation. Then the heap is turned so that the outside now becomes the inside, and in three or four days it will have heated all over and be ready for the frame, where a pit to receive it has been dug about two and a half feet deep if the garden is in a Northern area, two feet or less if farther South. Into this the fermenting manure must be firmly compacted and then covered with about six inches of good fine topsoil. Manure may also be banked around the outside of the frame to assist in the heating process. The sash is closed and the bed left for a few days until a thermometer plunged well down shows that the soil temperature has dropped to 75° or 80° F., when the seed may be sown.

HOTBED: ELECTRICALLY HEATED

For the farm home garden, where supplies of manure are readily available and without expense, the old-style hotbed may be satisfactory, but even there, if current is available, the convenience and the saving in time attendant on the electric hotbed often justify its installation. The initial cost is not high since the wire, cable, thermo-

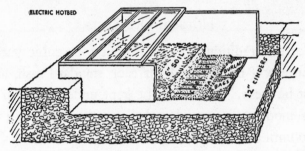

stat, and switch are all that need be purchased in addition to the cold frame. The cost of operation is also low, the consumption of electricity being from one and a half to two kilowatt hours per day for a single sash. One drawback is the possibility of breakdown in the supply of current, usually in time of severe weather when it is most needed. The frame must then be hastily and sufficiently covered in the hope of saving its contents from destruction.

The pit for an electric hotbed is dug about eighteen inches deep and a foot longer and wider than the frame it is to contain. To a depth of twelve inches it is filled with coarse cinders or furnace slag, which will also be packed round the sides of the frame for heat insulation. Over the cinders a layer of burlap is spread, then sand an inch deep, on which the heating cable is arranged in even, parallel rows about six and a half inches apart so that the warmth may be evenly distributed. This cable is an insulated wire with resistance of one half ohm per foot, sheathed in lead, and quite flexible; about thirty feet will be required per standard 6 × 3 ft. sash. The depth of soil over the cable will depend upon whether the plants are to be grown in it, which would require about six inches, or in flats laid on it, when two to three inches would be sufficient.

Hotbed: Piped Heat

When pipes from the heating system of the house can be extended to serve the hotbed, operation is both economical and inexpensive. The pipes, however, should not be laid in the midst of the soil, for if they are near the surface the heating will be dangerously uneven; if they are buried deeply, much of it will be wasted. The alternatives are an air space of six to nine inches below the bed in which the pipes are arranged in parallel rows about eighteen inches apart, or to run a single pipe around the inside walls above the soil level. It is, of course, essential that an efficient valve be provided for heat control, and it should be set in some readily accessible place inside the house.

Hotbed: from the Basement Window

A very satisfactory small hotbed, and most economical in operation, can be made if the home has a basement window with southern exposure. The construction of pit, sides, and sash will be the same as for a cold frame, but the walls must be high enough at the back to be above the basement window, whence they slope sharply to the front. They should be well caulked where they

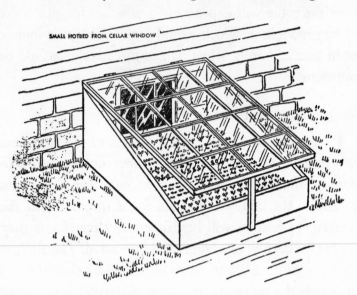

SMALL HOTBED FROM CELLAR WINDOW

join the house and earthed up at the sides to exclude wind and cold. The sash may be of the full standard type or smaller, as desired, and should be hinged at the top.

Warm air from the basement is admitted through the window, which is left open at night but may be closed on sunny days, and the sash raised for ventilation. While the temperature attained will not be so high in this simple frame as in a hotbed, it is likely to be a uniform warmth that will bring the young plants along very well and with the minimum of trouble.

HOTBED MANAGEMENT

In hotbed operation the two points that require most careful attention are ventilation and watering, in order to

secure, as nearly as possible, a relatively constant degree
of heat and humidity both for the progressive growth of
the plants and the avoidance of conditions favorable to
the organisms of damping-off. Since the plants in a hotbed are forced, they are apt to be tender and sensitive
both to chill and to attack. Overheating and lack of ventilation accentuate this condition and thus even on cold
days some ventilation is needed at the warmest hours.
The gardener's judgment must determine how much to
raise the sash and for how long, but it should be closed
again before the afternoon light begins to fade. Watering
will probably be required only occasionally, especially in
cloudy weather, and it should be done when the temperature is rising. The surface should afterward be stirred
if it shows any sign of caking, to secure proper soil aeration. Weeds inevitably show up even in the privacy of a
well-ordered frame but should never be allowed to make
any progress at any time, whether plants are being grown
in the frame or not.

CHAPTER VI

Preparing the Soil

SOIL TESTING

A very desirable preliminary to all the outdoor operations in the garden, and a particular necessity in the case of new vegetable plots, is a test to determine whether any additions to the soil are necessary in order that sufficient plant food may be available for the crops that are to be grown.

The first consideration is acidity, for an acid condition of the soil usually means that nitrates are low and phosphates in insoluble forms, therefore unavailable to plants, while aluminum, iron, and manganese compounds may be in more soluble compounds that are toxic in effect. If the soil is unduly alkaline, however, potash supplies are low; manganese, iron, and other minor elements may be locked up. Other deficiencies and necessary amendments will be indicated by analysis that may be made by the gardener himself with a soil-testing kit, which is a very interesting and informative piece of apparatus, or by his state agricultural experiment station, which will report to him in a few days, usually without charge.

In preparing a sample for the station, take five thin slices the full depth of a spade, one from near each corner of the plot and one from the center. From the middle of each slice take a strip about two inches wide, collecting in all about a pound of soil, and mix them all together. If one part of the garden is markedly different from the rest, a second sample may be necessary, but unless the area is very large this is unlikely. Addresses of the various state experiment stations are given in the appendix, and when the sample is sent, the gardener's name and address should be clearly written on the parcel. At the same time a letter should be sent asking for whatever advice is required; this should be made as brief and concise as is possible, at the same time giving all the facts, for the facilities of the station are likely to be busily employed at the time when most people ask for tests.

TIME TO BEGIN

Though the result of the test may to some extent condition procedure in preparing the soil, plowing or digging may be commenced as soon as the garden is sufficiently dry. A handful of earth may be taken and squeezed in the hand; if it crumbles readily on being released, it is in good working condition, but if it is wet and sticky it would tend to become lumpy and hard if worked, especially if it is at all heavy in texture.

DRAINAGE

If the only site available for the vegetable garden should, unhappily, be one that requires draining, this will be one of the first operations for attention. Vegetables cannot be grown in waterlogged soil, sour through lack of aeration and only made more so by applications of fertilizer.

Often what looks like a wet situation, where rain water collects and stands, can be remedied by digging deeply, breaking up the soil, and adding humus. Occasional saturated spots may be alleviated by digging sump holes three feet wide and three feet deep. Into these is first put a twelve-inch layer of stones, then a layer of sod with the grass side down to prevent soil from filling up the space between the stones. The remaining two feet is filled with topsoil. If more than that is necessary, a stone-filled ditch may suffice, but a tiled drain is much more desirable from every point of view.

An outlet for the drain is to be determined, and this may be an adjacent stream or pond but more often will be a blind well or sump hole filled with large stones. It may be assumed that the drain will take off surplus water from ten feet on either side of it, and thus one line is likely to be sufficient in most home gardens, but the drainage area can be extended by lateral branches. The trench should be dug two feet deep and with a gentle fall to the outlet, the topsoil to be thrown on one side, subsoil on the other. In this are laid the drain tiles, which are short lengths of straight earthenware pipe without any overlapping flange; the end of one length must be as close as possible to the next. The upper end of the first length should be surrounded by large stones and gravel to prevent the entry of soil which might block the drain; and for the same purpose cinders may be placed at least at each joint. As the laying proceeds each section must be carefully bedded so that all of its length rests on firm earth. Finally the subsoil, or a little less than was taken out, allowing for the pipe, is thrown into the trench and the topsoil restored.

It will be some time before the water that is soaking the near-by area finds its way to the drain, but the effects will be cumulative and apparent in due course.

PLOWING

It is usually necessary to have the large home garden of, say, 50 × 100 ft. or more, plowed and harrowed by animal- or tractor-drawn equipment; gardens of medium size may well be worked with the plow and harrow or cultivator attachments of the wheel hoe, while for small plots the spade and rake suffice. Heavy soils should be plowed or spaded in late fall and left rough throughout the winter for the beneficial action of the elements; and if the garden is on a slope this is good practice for any soil, to prevent erosion, unless a cover crop is standing. Otherwise light soils may be left until spring, and when plowing is done then, harrowing should follow the same day; similarly any plot that is spaded in spring should be raked immediately afterward.

DEPTH

The depth of plowing or spading will largely depend on the depth of the topsoil. For good tillage, eight or nine inches is desirable, and if the topsoil is much shallower than this, it can be gradually deepened by plowing just a little lower each season, or by using a subsoil plow to break up the substratum. This may be done more speedily with the spade by double digging or trenching. Such work is preferably done in the fall.

SPADES ARE TRUMPS

Plowing is very well for the ample garden and the only practical means of turning the soil on a farm; but digging, whether with spade or spading fork, still re-

DIGGING STILL REMAINS THE GARDENER'S
MOST EFFECTIVE METHOD OF TILLAGE

mains the gardener's most effective method of deep tillage. In this way the soil can be thoroughly broken up
and aerated, with great benefit to the manifold reactions
that go on in it and to its moisture content; if the topsoil
is deep, its undersurface is often rich and can be brought
up; or if it is shallow, the depth can be increased by
improving the inert subsoil.

When digging, except in shallow topsoil, the full depth
of the blade or tines should be thrust into the earth
almost vertically rather than at an angle. This gives
better leverage and cuts deeper, with less stooping and
effort. The bite taken, however, should not be too thick
and should be turned over before it leaves the tool, then
sliced where it falls.

It is usually advisable to dig only as much as can be
raked and planted on the same day, especially in sunny or
windy weather.

DOUBLE DIGGING

Even with a good spade, physical stamina, and a will-
ing spirit, digging means work; not necessarily unpleasant
or exhausting, but nonetheless work, and its effort can
be alleviated if it is planned and done methodically.

If manure or compost is available, dispose it conveniently in small lumps on the plot, and proceed to open
up a trench one spit deep, two or three spits wide—spit,
the old name for a spade, meaning now the area of the
blade. The topsoil from this trench is put on the outside

of the plot, to be moved to the other end when the last stretch is dug. If manure is being spread, or trash turned under, fork it into the bottom of the trench and cover it with the soil from the second trench, adding any commercial fertilizer that may be required; repeat this procedure until the last trench is filled with soil from the first. This will make the raking much easier to do, and there will be no loose straws and untidy pieces sticking up when it is finished.

TRENCHING

Where the topsoil is deep, trenching is the ideal method of bringing the lower level of it to the surface and working the whole into a deep, mellow bed. The first trench is made about two feet wide and two spits deep instead of one as in double digging. Manure or whatever enrichment is available is thrown into the bottom of the trench, and over this is spread soil one spit deep from the adjoining two-foot strip. More enrichment is now added and the trench is filled up with the second digging of the adjoining strip. Thus the soil is turned upside down from trench to trench.

When the topsoil is shallow, a modified form of trenching may be worked. In this case the subsoil is broken up as well as possible and manure is added to it but only a very small portion of it, say about an inch, is brought to the surface and added to the topsoil that is moved from trench to trench. A few seasons of such organized

digging will effect a very great improvement in a poor
and shallow soil.

RIDGING

A profitable practice before laying away the spade for
that season is to dig the garden into ridges, incorporating
and covering any manure or other organic matter available. These ridges are purposely left rough so that they
may be well weathered, while in the furrows between
them the rain and snow will soak the soil. The maximum
surface is thus exposed, and in spring the ridges dry
more quickly, when they need only to be leveled off and
harrowed or raked before planting.

FINAL PULVERIZING AND SMOOTHING
WITH A STRONG STEEL RAKE

RAKING

Though the edge of the spade or fork may have been
well used to break up all lumps of soil as dug and though
the wheel plow may have been followed by the cultivator prongs, there remains a final pulverizing and
smoothing, which are best effected with a strong steel

rake but supplemented by a heavy or mattock hoe if stubborn clods are still to be broken up. In average soils, however, the back of the rake will be sufficient for this purpose, and most of the work will be done with the teeth in working the soil down into good tilth, that is, fine-grained physical condition. The raking should by no means be only on the surface: the teeth must go deep enough to dispose of all lumps for a depth of several inches and should then move evenly through the seed-bed, which is finally smoothed off with the back of the rake.

SOWING

Before seeds are sown or plants moved from the frame or flat, a row for them is to be marked out, not merely for the sake of symmetrical appearance, but for convenience in the subsequent work of cultivation. A pair of stakes, a length of garden line, and a yardstick will give the preliminary mark along which the point of a Warren hoe, or the corner of another, may be drawn to make a drill.

The old rule for depth of sowing was that the seed should be covered with a thickness of soil equal to twice its diameter, but too many factors are involved for any such generalization to be accurate. Thus planting will be deeper in a light or sandy soil than in a heavy or clay loam, due to the greater moisture content of the latter; and for a similar reason seeds are planted deeper in sum-

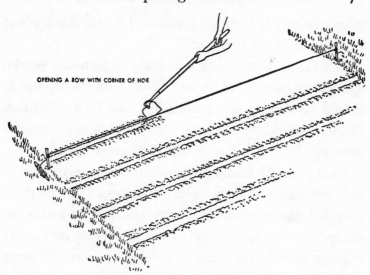

OPENING A ROW WITH CORNER OF HOE

mer than in spring. In proportion to their size, large seeds are planted deeper than small, some of which are barely covered. The only good rule, therefore, is to become acquainted with the particular requirements of each species and balance these with the conditions of soil and season.

When the seed has been sown and suitably covered, it is of great importance that the soil around it be firmed down, which in most cases can be done with the sole of the shoe, though for small seeds with light coverage it may be better to do this essential task with a piece of board or the back of the spade. It is assumed, of course, that the soil will not be so wet as to stick to the shoe.

If this is neglected, the seed may not receive sufficient moisture to enable germination; or if it does germinate, it will be unable to make progress if its rootlets are not in intimate contact with soil.

Small seeds planted just below the surface may need a sprinkle of water before and after germination, but it should be very gently applied lest they be washed out. If there should be danger of this from heavy rain, the row may be covered with burlap or other old bags.

Soon after the seedlings appear, it will be necessary to thin out many of them. This work should not be postponed, because crowded plants grow leggy and spindling—a bad beginning in life from which they may never recover entirely. In some cases two or more thinnings will be advisable, always leaving the strongest plants in the row. The soil should be moist when thinning out is done, and care should be taken that soil is firmed around the plants left standing.

TRANSPLANTING

The shock of being moved out to the garden may greatly check the growth of a plant, and efforts should be made to minimize it as much as possible. Therefore they first undergo a gradual process of hardening-off by giving them more and more exposure to the outside air. If the plants are in a flat, this may be blocked out about ten days before transplanting by cutting lengthwise and crosswise down to the bottom, thus limiting each plant to its own square and giving it an opportunity to develop root branches in lieu of ends that may have been cut off

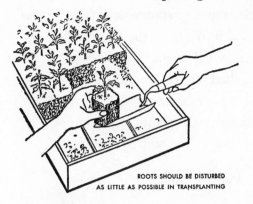

ROOTS SHOULD BE DISTURBED
AS LITTLE AS POSSIBLE IN TRANSPLANTING

PLANT PUDDLED IN WITH
STARTER SOLUTION

in the blocking out. Again if they are lifted from a frame or seedbed, a good ball of earth should be taken with them, so that the roots may always be covered and suffer no more disturbance than is necessary.

Before bringing out the plants, make holes for them of the proper depth and proper distance apart in the row. They may look rather far apart from one another at this stage, but they will grow.

STARTER SOLUTION

In recent years commercial growers have been adding a little plant food to the water used at transplanting, with very successful results in eliminating wilting and starting the plants on new growth very rapidly. Much experimentation has shown that a complete fertilizer is best and that it should be high in phosphorus, as 13-26-13, which is recommended to be used at the rate of two ounces to a bucketful of water, the quantity to be increased if the fertilizer analysis is lower; a large handful of 5-10-5, for example, and a teaspoonful of lime. Some of this solution is poured into a hole, the plant is then set in the little puddle somewhat deeper than it was in the flat, and the soil is packed firmly around it. When the row has been planted it may be watered with the solution and, so far from burning the plants, as might possibly have been anticipated, the effect will be beneficial.

Protection

Transplanting is best done on a cloudy, cool day, and if there should be bright sunshine within the next few days, the more tender plants may need to be shaded to prevent them from wilting. Paper covers, either those sold for the purpose or homemade cones, preferably of glassine or waxed paper to admit light, are often used to protect early seedlings from extremes of temperature, rain, wind, and danger from birds or insects. To allow ventilation, a one-inch slit may be cut in the cover, on

SHINGLE AS A PLANT PROTECTOR

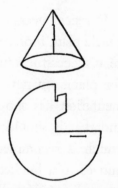

PAPER CONE AS A PLANT PROTECTOR

the opposite side to the prevailing wind, and gradually enlarged until the cover can be finally removed.

WATERING

Water is a vital necessity to the growth of plants and only if it is in sufficient supply throughout the season can yield and quality from the vegetable garden be obtained. In some parts of the country no irrigation will be needed in hot weather, though recent investigation shows that in relatively cool and humid areas water may profitably be added more frequently than has been thought necessary, so that plants may not be checked by even short periods of dry weather. In other parts, some form of additional water supply must always be provided, and overhead sprinklers are a feature of the large gardens and commercial growers' farms. Subirrigation by water pumped into tile drains is used but rarely, and surface irrigation by water conveyed in furrows is more practicable.

For the home gardener with a medium-sized plot the hose and the watering can usually provide all that is required. Practice and experience are the only guides to their use and no rules can be offered except one: watering should either be done thoroughly or not at all. Not so thoroughly as to wash the nutrients out of the soil, but enough to soak well down around the roots of the plants and further. To this end a rotary sprinkler on the hose pipe is very effective. Light sprinkling tends to cake the soil and if repeated often enough leads to the formation of roots near the surface where they are likely to be burned in hot weather.

CULTIVATION

However well a gardener has prepared his soil, weeds will spring up to fight his plants for it. The seeds of some of them lie in the ground for many years awaiting a favorable opportunity for germination; others are carried by the wind or dropped by birds, even carried in on the soil that clings to shoes.

The yield of a garden may be reduced one half or more by a small crop of weeds, and in addition to this competition they often act as hosts for fungous diseases and insect pests. Therefore the cultivator and the hoe

WHEEL CULTIVATOR USED BETWEEN ROWS

must be in continual use throughout the growing season, preventing the weeds from ever getting to be more than an inch high, at which stage they are easily killed by shallow cultivation, with additional benefits to the garden plants by way of soil aeration and the creation of a dust mulch which prevents the escape of much moisture by evaporation.

Emphasis should be laid on the word shallow. The best results are likely to be attained with the scuffle or D-hoe, which cuts the weeds just below the surface of the soil and thus avoids damage to plant roots.

A new doctrine is that the dust mulch is ineffective in preventing evaporation and that instead of old-fashioned cultivation a litter mulch of straw, hay, or salt hay should be spread. Proponents of this method claim that its benefits are not confined to the repression of weeds and the retention of soil moisture. As plant food in the upper strata is made available, the soil bacteria increase and there is less work to be done. But most gardeners have found the dust mulch sufficiently effective and will be unlikely to relinquish the hoe.

Cultivation should begin almost as soon as the garden is planted, and even if the garden is relatively free of weeds it is always necessary in order to keep the soil in good tilth. It is usually better not to cultivate on wet days: among other and more obvious objections there is sometimes a risk of spreading plant diseases when the foliage is wet.

Mulch paper has some value in keeping down weeds and may bring considerable ease of mind to the gardener who wishes to go on vacation, or for other reasons has to abandon the hoe temporarily.

CULTIVATION

WITH HOE

THE VEGETABLES

VEGETABLE PLANTING CHART

	Depth to Cover Plants (inches)	Space between Rows (in.)	Space between Plants (in.)	Days Required to Prod. Crop Ready for Use	Time to Plant in Open Ground — South	Time to Plant in Open Ground — North
Asparagus	Plants, 4 in.	40	20	Plants 2 years	Early Spring	Early Spring
Beans—Bush	1½	24	2	60 to 80	Mid-spring, Sept.–Oct.	May–June
—Pole	2	36	3	80 to 100	March–May	Late Spring
Beans, Lima—Bush	2	24	3–4	70 to 90	Spring	Late Spring
—Pole	2	36	3	80 to 100	Spring	April–August
Beet	½	18	2–3	60 to 80	Feb.–April, Sept.–Oct.	Spring
Broccoli	¼	30	24	70	Spring & Fall	May–June
Brussels Sprouts	¼	30	24	100	Spring	March–June
Cabbage	¼	24	18–24	70 to 120	Oct.–Nov., Feb.–April	April–June
Carrot	¼	18	2–4	60	Mar. & Apr., Sept.–Nov.	April–June
Cauliflower	—	36	24	60 to 80	Jan. & Feb., Sept.–Oct.	May–June
Celery	—	36	6	90 to 120	Aug.–Oct.	
Chinese Cabbage	¼	24	12	70	Spring & Fall	Spring & Fall
Collard	¼	36	24	80 to 100	Spring & Fall	Summer
Corn, Sweet	1	30	12	80 to 100	Feb.–April	May–July
Cucumber	¼	60	3 to hill	60 to 80	Feb.–April	April–July
Eggplant	—	36	24	80 to 100	Feb.–April, Sept.–Nov.	April–May

Endive	24	1/8	10-12	80	Feb.-April	April-August
Kale	24	1/4	18	100	Oct.-Feb.	Aug.-Sept., Mar.-Apr.
Leek	24	1/8	6	100	May-Sept.	Mar.-May
Lettuce	18	1/8	10	50 to 80	Sept.-Mar.	Mar. & Sept.
Muskmelon	60	—	3 to hill	90 to 120	Feb.-April	April-June
Onion, Bulb	15	—	4	90 to 120	Sept.-Oct., Mar.-April	April-May
Onion, Bunching	15	—	1-2	50 to 60	Early Spring	March to May
Parsnip	24	1/4	4	120		Spring
Peas	24	1½	1½	60 to 80	Sept.-Oct., Oct.-Nov.	Mar.-May
Pepper	36	—	24	80 to 100	Early Spring	May-June
Potatoes	36	4	12	100	Jan.-April, Sept.-Oct.	March-June
Pumpkin	72	1/2	3 to hill	120	April-May	May-June
Radish	18	1/4	1-3	25 to 60	Sept.-April	March-Sept.
Rhubarb	48	5	48	2 years	——	Early Spring
Spinach	15	1/2	5	50 to 60	Sept.-Feb.	Sept. or very early Spring
Spinach, N. Zealand	36	1	20	70 to 80		Spring
Squash, Summer	48	1	36	60 to 80	Spring	April-July
Sweet Potatoes	48	3	20	120	Spring	May-June
Swiss Chard	24	1/2	12	60	April-June	Spring
Tomato	36-48	—	36	70 to 90	Spring	May-June
Turnip	15	1/8	5	50 to 80	Aug.-Nov.	April-Aug.
Rutabaga or Swede Turnip	24	1/8	7	90 to 100	Aug.-Nov.	May-June

CHAPTER VII

The Vegetables

ARTICHOKE

BUR ARTICHOKE GLOBE ARTICHOKE

Cynara scolymus

This great thistle-like plant is hardly to be admitted a member of the garden company in America, since it requires a large amount of space and is ill-adapted to the extremes of climate prevalent in most parts of the country. Where it can be grown, however, it yields a succulent dish from the fleshy bases of the scales, or involucre bracts, of its unopened flowering heads, in each of which is also a heart, the receptacle from which flowers arise, esteemed among epicures.

The chief center of production for the produce markets is in California, between San Francisco and Los Angeles, but it is also grown commercially in places on the Gulf coast and South Atlantic shore, in all such cases as a winter crop. These areas are relatively free from frost, while summer heat is tempered by proximity to the ocean and attendant fogs. Summer heat causes the buds, or heads, to open early, with consequent loss of size and edible quality.

Artichoke is thus seen to be a cool-weather plant, but it is occasionally raised with fair success in the Eastern states as far north as Massachusetts, where it is cut down in late fall, the crown covered with a bushel basket or a box, and manure mulch piled over and around this, but not directly on the crown.

It is well that there are climatic limitations to its growth, for when it escapes from cultivation in favorable circumstances it may become a troublesome weed, as has happened in parts of California.

The plant is a herbaceous perennial; that is, it dies down to the roots each year after seed production and grows again the following season, rising to a height of four or five feet and spreading to an even greater width. After the third year, however, there begins a marked decrease in the number and quality of the buds, or heads, for which it is primarily grown, and new plantings are made from shoots which arise at the base of old plants. Seed is very rarely used, since it cannot be relied upon to produce plants true to type; instead, the shoots or suckers are set out about six feet apart in the rows, which are eight feet apart. A few buds may be produced in the same season, but in the following year both the main stalk and lateral branches will be in full bearing. The best head is the one at the end of a stalk, but many others are borne, maturing at different times. They are to be cut just before they are due to open into flower, leaving an inch or two of stem below the base. Two types of head are grown in California: one, a somewhat flattened globe shape with broad scales, known as French; the other, more blunt-cone shaped, known as Italian and regarded as the better, both for yield and for convenience in packing.

The artichoke is a specialized form of cardoon, from which it was developed many centuries ago, possibly on the Barbary coast. Passages in the classical authors of Greece and Rome sometimes quoted as applying to it would more properly be referred to cardoon. It may be surmised that it was selected for large heads in the days of Arab power; a record exists of their cultivating it in Spain in the twelfth century, and the word artichoke is derived from the Spanish-Arabic *al-kharshúf*, the rough-skinned, Spanish *alcachofa*, Italian *articiocco*, and thence to English in such earlier forms as *archecock*.

ASPARAGUS

Asparagus officinalis

When a gardener cuts the first substantial asparagus stalks of his own planting and growing he may be said to have graduated in the art of vegetable culture. He has shown his skill and demonstrated that his interest is not the fleeting enthusiasm of a single season but is supported by the patience of all true gardeners, so that he is content to work for a deferred reward and looks forward to producing for many years one of the finer luxuries of the table.

Asparagus is not a difficult crop; indeed it will grow after a fashion almost anywhere if it does not have to stand in a waterlogged or sour spot. But it cannot be cropped quickly and it requires lots of room. It is for the permanent garden and there, with reasonable care, it will endure for twenty years, providing an attractive green background through the summer months after the cutting season is over.

Space Required

To plot the necessary space, allow a dozen plants for each member of the family, which should provide enough to serve asparagus twice a week while it lasts, with some over for guests or gifts. Sixty plants is a good number for the average home. Set at eighteen inches apart, a hundred feet of row will be required, or three rows of thirty-three feet. If these rows are four feet apart, the area of the plot will be approximately forty by fifteen feet, allowing for the space surrounding the outer plants.

Location

This space should be at one end or side of the garden, with other perennials, to be out of the way of seasonal operations on the annual vegetables, but it is essential

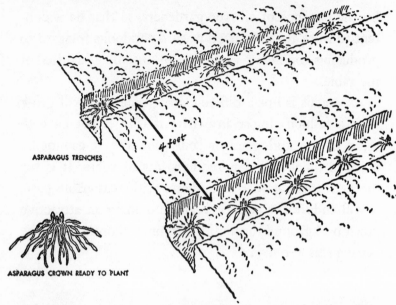

ASPARAGUS TRENCHES

ASPARAGUS CROWN READY TO PLANT

that the site selected must be well drained and for preference it should be light in texture, as sandy loam soils
warm up earlier and asparagus is an early crop.

Preparation

It is desirable that preparation of the plot should begin
during the season before planting in order to get rid of
the worst of the weeds, which are difficult to control in
a young asparagus bed, and to get the soil into good
tilth, free of rocks and stones that might lead to crooked
stalks. As it is intended to stand for twenty years with
only shallow cultivation after the plants have been set,
now is the time to fit it thoroughly and enrich it deeply
with manure or compost, and if there is one place more

than another where trenching is beneficial, it is right here. Growing and turning under a green manure crop are also very helpful. Liming may be necessary, as asparagus does not thrive on acid soil, and enough ground limestone may be worked in to bring the reaction to pH 6.5. The quantity required should be determined by test.

The final fitting of the plot, by pulverizing with harrow or hand tools, working in a couple of pounds of complete fertilizer per hundred square feet, and firming down afterward, is to be done as early as possible in the season so that the crowns which are going to be planted, and which are on sale at that time, will not be lying around instead of setting about their protracted business.

What to Plant

Although asparagus can be raised from seed, to do so would add more work and another year to the already long enough time required to raise a crop, so the planting of one-year-old crowns, or roots, is the better method for the home gardener. These can be had at the seed stores and are quite inexpensive, but are not usually graded as to size. Therefore it is well to order a hundred and select the sixty largest and stoutest for the planting. A few from the best of the discards may be temporarily set in some unwanted part of the garden as spare parts in case a replacement is needed in the rows. To the compost heap with the remainder.

Asparagus is dioecious, that is, some plants are male, the others female, and it is sometimes suggested that male plants be selected because they produce more spears. The increase is slight, however, and the spears somewhat smaller. In addition, only in the long growing season of the South is blossoming achieved in the first year from seed, and anything that might be in favor of male plants is offset by having to wait for second-year crowns, which suffer too much through being dug up.

Planting

Mark out and open up trenches two feet wide and at a distance apart of four feet from center to center. The old method of digging deeply and packing in manure is obsolete, fortunately for the gardener, since it is recognized that asparagus roots spread horizontally rather than downward, this being also the reason for wide spacing.

The trenches are made six or eight inches deep and, in order to prevent pockets of water below the crowns, with a ridge down the center, or a slight hump at each plant on which the crown is set with the buds up and the roots spread out radically around it. A distance of two feet apart makes good allowance for their growth, but this may be a little less if space is lacking.

The first covering of the roots will be only two or three inches so that growth may start more quickly, and as buds appear above the surface more soil is worked down from the sides, at the same time destroying any weeds that appear, so that before the end of the season the trench is filled. The stalks will be thin and spindly but should make plentiful growth of the finely cut ferny branchlets which serve as leaves (the true leaves being merely scales on the spears), where food is manufactured and sent down to the roots to be stored up there for use in the early part of the following season.

An Older Method

The method of planting described above is now generally accepted, but the old-fashioned asparagus bed is still occasionally made for economy of space. A bed five feet wide is dug eighteen inches deep and packed with manure to the depth of nine inches over which is spread three inches of soil. The plants are set fifteen to eighteen inches apart in three rows, the first of which is a foot from the side of the bed; the other two, eighteen inches apart. This close planting calls for plenty of fertilizer as time goes on, and the bed is not likely either to produce as satisfactory yields or to endure as long as the newer, more open rows.

Cultivation and Care

It is important that weeds be relentlessly kept down around asparagus, especially in its early stages, until the plants shade the soil, for if the weeds are allowed to establish themselves, deeper cultivation will be required to eliminate them, with the risk of damage to the spreading asparagus roots. The old practice of applying common salt to asparagus beds no doubt did some good by inhibiting weeds, though as plant food it was of little, if any, service.

Asparagus can use plenty of fertilizer, the effects of which will be seen in the size of the following season's spears. Two pounds per one hundred square feet worked in all over the planting will be beneficial, a ratio of 1-2-2 being best for sandy soils and 1-2-1 for better loam soils. These ratios would mean such analyses as 5-10-10 and 5-10-5. If manure or compost is available it may be spread and lightly dug in, to avoid damaging the roots, at the end of the growing season. At this time the tops are to be cut and thrown on the compost heap, but care must be taken not to do this too soon or valuable food material on its way down to the roots for storage will be lost. Do not scatter the seeds, for they may come up as weeds.

Harvest

No cutting will be possible in the same season as planting, and in the following season only a little, perhaps none, but in the third season three cuttings, one a week or so, can usually be made from each plant, when the spears are about six inches above ground. In later years asparagus will be on the menu three or four times a week, until thin stalks appear and thus show that the roots have yielded the surplus of their store, when cutting must cease.

The spear is held in one hand; a long, sharp, thin-bladed knife, or a special asparagus knife, cuts it about two inches below the surface. Great care must be taken, inserting the blade almost vertically and angling it at the right point, not to injure the tops of other growing but still unseen spears. Some gardeners prefer to cut at or just below the surface, promptly covering the stump.

A little mound is sometimes thrown up over each plant before cutting begins, with a view to increasing the diameter of the spears, but this is not essential.

Insect Pests

The common asparagus beetle and its relative the twelve-spotted asparagus beetle are the chief enemies. Both are about a quarter inch long; the first is blue-black with three white spots and an orange margin on each wing case; the second is orange with six black spots on each wing case. Both make their appearance from adjacent trash where they have wintered, just as the young shoots appear, and feed on the tips, producing unsightly holes and discoloration. Later they eat both foliage and stems, seriously injuring the plants.

Dusting the tips with .75 per cent rotenone is effective and harmless; after the cutting season the plants may be dusted occasionally with rotenone or fifteen parts of calcium arsenate mixed with eighty-five parts of slaked lime or, if the beetles are infrequent, they may be shaken off into a can of water topped with kerosene.

Disease-Resistant Varieties

Asparagus has a long history, of which the most important chapter, from the modern grower's point of view, was written in America thirty to forty years ago. Crops in the Eastern states had been devastated by asparagus rust when the late Dr. J. B. Norton of the U.S. Department of Agriculture began a program of breeding for disease-resistance in infested soil at Concord, Massachusetts, where he grew many varieties, collected from all over the world. In 1910 a tall, resistant male plant which he had named Washington was crossed with Martha, a female plant, and the result was Martha Washington, a notably rust-resistant variety. Similarly Washington was crossed with Mary, a giant female of the same variety as Martha, and thus was produced what is by far the most extensively planted variety in America today: Mary Washington.

Let the grower make sure that his crowns are of the Mary Washington variety and he may look forward to superb stalks with little risk of trouble from the once-dreaded rust, for which no completely effective control has ever been found.

BEANS

Many are the references to beans in ancient literature, and there is evidence that they were used for food in the Bronze Age of Europe some thousands of years ago. But those were very different species from our common or garden bean, the Lima bean, and the runner bean, of which the Old World knew nothing.

One of the first things noted by Columbus when he got here was that beans he saw in the fields were unlike any he had seen before, and it shortly became apparent, as other parts of America were visited by explorers, that they were grown from north to south. Seeds were taken back, and before long the new beans had found such widespread popularity that they were being grown in Africa and Asia as well as Europe. So common did they become that their American nativity was forgotten, and —as may be seen in gardening books of the past generation—they were commonly regarded as native to Asia.

Some beans returned to America much improved by their residence abroad, notably the Refugee, which derives its name from the Huguenots, who brought it with them when they fled here in thousands about the beginning of the seventeenth century.

Indeed, whatever improvement took place in the common bean until comparatively recent years was largely due to chance field crosses or the selection of better plants for seed, especially in Europe. But some sixty or seventy years ago the late Calvin N. Keeney, a seed grower of LeRoy, New York, became interested in the idea of a bean without the fibrous string that used to be such a nuisance. Season after season he pursued his quest, until the new variety was eventually developed. Then it was turned over to his friend, the late W. Atlee Burpee, for introduction to the public, and since 1896 Burpee's Stringless Green Pod has been widely grown in American gardens. Keeney went on to produce other stringless varieties, both green pod and wax pod, and later workers have added others, so that now the term "string bean" is practically an obsolete survival of older days and should be abolished in favor of "snap bean."

Lima beans· take their name from the city of Lima, Peru, whence Capt. John Harris of the U.S. Navy carried seed to plant on his farm at Chester, New York, in 1824, after which they gained much attention; but beans of the Lima type had been grown in the South before then. All these were of the pole type; the bush Limas have been known for only about fifty years.

The runner beans form the third group of American origin. Of these the scarlet-flowered varieties are occasionally grown for ornament in this country, but in Europe they are popular for table use and pods are grown a foot or more in length, though of rather rough quality at that stage.

Bush Beans

Phaseolus vulgaris

No American garden, however small, is complete without its rows of beans. They will grow almost anywhere provided they have warmth with a reasonable amount of moisture and of plant food in the soil. Under such conditions and with proper protection from pests they produce abundantly and, being legumes, tend to leave more nitrogen in the soil.

In habit of growth there are two types: bush and climbing or pole. Many varieties of both are· available, some with green pods, a lesser number with wax pods; and of both these the new and better varieties are stringless. Others are not grown for their pods but for shelled beans, eaten green when immature or dry after full growth. These are not now so popular in the garden as they were in bygone days and are largely the same varieties as then were grown.

Varieties

GREEN PODS: This is by far the most popular type and the choice of varieties is correspondingly great. A preference may be felt as to the shape and shade of the pods, and of those that are round in section Tendergreen may be ranked first—a hardy and productive variety with dark green, stringless pods. Next would come Giant Stringless and Burpee's Stringless.

If oval pods are preferred, Stringless Black Valentine is of fine flavor; the term "Black" refers to the seeds, not the pods, which are dark green. Of the flat-podded sorts Bountiful has long been the most popular though it must be picked young, when the pods are light green, as it later develops some fiber. A new variety of the same type, Plentiful, seems likely to replace it. In many Southern gardens Tennessee Green Pod is highly regarded for its large, flat pods if picked early.

WAX PODS: The best of the round-podded type is Pencil Pod, but its seeds are black. Brittle Wax has white seeds. Sure Crop, sometimes called Bountiful Wax, is a very thrifty and productive plant with flat oval pods; its seeds are black. Golden Wax has white seeds with a little mottling, but is not quite of such good eating quality.

SHELLING BEANS: Dwarf Horticultural is the variety most generally used; its alternative name of Speckled Cranberry indicates the sort of shelled bean it produces. The pods are good as snap beans if eaten young. French's Horticultural is very similar but with considerably longer pods, which take about two weeks more to mature.

Beans for Dry Use: These are nowadays chiefly used by the commercial houses though there are still some thrifty gardeners who plant them for use in winter months. White Kidney, Red Kidney, White Marrowfat, and the small Navy Pea-Bean are standard varieties.

POLE BEANS

GREEN PODS: Being a much larger plant, the pole bean can bear many more pods than can the low bush. But more space per plant is required, and the providing of poles or other support such as trellis means more work for the gardener. In general, therefore, the bush beans are much more popular. Yet that old favorite, Kentucky Wonder, well rewards the gardener for his pains by its clusters of long, curved green pods. These are to be picked directly they reach full size and not allowed to grow more mature as they then become somewhat fibrous. In the South, where pole beans are much more popular than in the North, Ideal Market, black-seeded, and McCaslan, white-seeded, are frequently planted.

WAX PODS: This type is but little grown and the pods are not usually of such good quality as the bush wax varieties. Kentucky Wonder Wax, the best known of the varieties, is brown-seeded; Golden Cluster is white-seeded and sometimes saved for dry beans after its pods pass the edible stage.

LIMA BEANS

Phaseolus limensis

What has been said above applies equally to Lima beans, except that they are even more intolerant of cold, wet soils and take longer to ripen; some Northern gardeners, therefore, start them indoors three or four weeks before the garden is likely to be thoroughly warmed. In sowing, the seeds of the larger bush varieties are usually set a little farther apart—three to four inches—and probably two plantings will be sufficient. The seeds are to be set with the eye down and there should be enough soil moisture to induce germination.

The pole Limas are somewhat heavy plants and are often allowed one pole per plant, a good method being three poles set wigwam fashion and tied at the top. Being braced thus, they do not need to be set deeper in the ground than six or eight inches.

Bush Varieties: There are two types: first, the large-seeded or potato Lima, which is largely favored because of its higher yield (under good growing conditions), flavor, and being easier to shell—Fordhook Bush is perhaps the best one; second, the baby Lima, known in the South as a butter bean—of which Henderson's Bush is the best known. Its beans are small, green when young, but at later stages both green and white beans occur. A new strain, recently introduced as Clark's Bush, produces only green beans at the fresh picking stage.

For the South, Jackson Wonder is a good variety of the butter-bean type, as it sets pods better in hot, dry conditions; its small beans are colored and strongly flavored.

Pole Varieties: Here the same two types occur, the small-seeded or, in the South, butter bean, and the large-seeded or potato Lima. Of the first, the exemplar is Sieva or Small White, a very ancient variety; of the second, King of the Garden.

Preparation

Beans will make the best of whatever soil they have, but that best will be much better if the rows have been well prepared. The soil must be well drained; it should be in good tilth, well worked over and free of clods, especially in view of the fact that the young plants bend their cotyledons, or seed leaves, up through it. A certain degree of acidity will be tolerated, and liming is not recommended unless the *p*H reaction is below 5.5. Commercial fertilizer, for preference somewhat low in nitrogen content, such as 5-10-10 analysis, is usually added at the rate of two and a half pounds per hundred feet of row. This should be thoroughly well distributed in the soil, as the germinating seed is very susceptible to injury from it. Experienced growers, therefore, prefer to supply it in a strip about three inches away from the row and two inches deep; similarly in a circle around pole beans.

Beans need phosphorus and potash more than nitrogen, much of which they derive from the by-product of bacteria growing in nodules on their roots, and excess nitrogen may lead to overdevelopment of foliage and scarcity of pods. Some of the bacteria are likely to be present in the soil, but if beans have never been grown there before, the seed may be shaken with a culture of the correct strain of bacteria obtainable cheaply at any good horticultural store.

Sowing

The soil must be warm before beans are planted, and as there often is warm weather before the average date of the last frost, gardeners usually make a first sowing of bush beans then, taking a chance on having to replace it if the frost does come. Some, indeed, in their eagerness to get an early start, soak the seed overnight, but cold, wet soil is likely to nullify any advantage there may be in this practice.

A row of about a hundred feet in all, throughout the season, will provide plenty of beans for a family of four or five and one pound of seed will be ample for sowing. This might perhaps be divided into twelve ounces of green pod and four ounces of wax pod.

The rate of planting may vary somewhat with the nature of the soil and the bush size of the selected variety but, on the average, two inches apart in the row, an inch and a half deep, and the rows two feet apart will be found satisfactory. Some growers incline to double rows, but this excludes sunlight and at the same time encourages pests. Others claim that bush beans in hills of three or four plants each produce larger pods, but the single row is by far the most general.

Sowing is not done all at once but in lengths of about twelve feet at intervals of ten days or two weeks until between two and three months before frost is expected. Thus fresh and flavorsome beans may be had all summer for the table and supplies will be ready for canning at any time convenient for that operation.

Pole beans are usually sown a little later than the first bush beans and in hills, not rows, unless trellis is used for them to climb upon. The hills are three to four feet apart

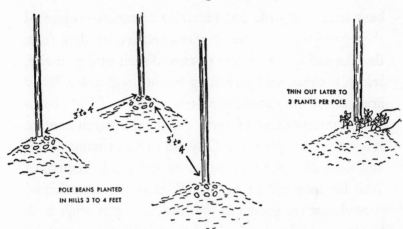

THIN OUT LATER TO
3 PLANTS PER POLE

3' to 4'

3' to 4'

POLE BEANS PLANTED
IN HILLS 3 TO 4 FEET

each way and five or six seeds set in each, to be thinned out later to three plants per pole. The poles should be set just before the seed, about eighteen inches below the surface and six feet above it; they should be rough, to provide a better hold for the climbing plants.

EDIBLE SOYBEANS

Soja max

Though soybeans have been grown in China for thousands of years, the crop is relatively a new one in North America, and only in recent years have we become aware of its immense potentialities not only to agriculture but as a source of raw material for industry. In addition, varieties of agreeable flavor have been introduced for garden culture and table use as shelled beans. Despite our innate conservatism in matters of food, these varieties have attracted wide and favorable attention because of their hardiness, very heavy yield, relative freedom from diseases and specific insect pests, and their eating quality, which is enhanced by pleasing bright green color. They are said to have twice the protein content of Lima beans and four times that of eggs, though the starch content is less than one per cent. They are rich in vitamins A, B, and G, with some C, superior to spinach in respect of available iron and to cow's milk in respect of calcium.

Soybeans are grown in the garden, just as other bush beans would be; in the kitchen they have one defect, which is that they are not so easy to shell as Lima beans. Shelling is made very much easier, however, by pouring boiling water over them; after standing in this for five minutes, the beans may be squeezed out at the end of the pod, not the side.

The earliest variety and most widely adapted, especially to the more northerly states, is Giant Green, which requires about eighty days from planting to picking; the latest is Higan, a month later and therefore better suited to the South. Between these are several other varieties of differing maturities and quite possibly, as with the field soybeans, better adapted to one district than another.

Cultivation

Weeds must be kept out of the bean rows and cultivation is very necessary, but it must be done with two safeguards in mind. One is that beans are shallow-rooted and may be injured by deep hoeing or cultivator prongs. The other is that the spores of anthracnose and other diseases may be easily distributed when the foliage is wet, and therefore beans should be left alone when rain or dew has wet the leaves. The first use of the hoe may be needed even before the plants appear; if the top surface of the soil has become caked through watering or rain it should be gently scuffled to make easier for the young seedlings the upward thrust to their new world.

Diseases

Bush beans are subject to several diseases, for which the general control measures are the planting of disease-free seed, pulling up and burning infected plants at once, and avoidance of the bean rows when they are wet. Anthracnose is a fungous disease, unknown in the West, which causes dark, sunken, more or less circular spots on the pods through which it grows to infect the seeds. On the stems and leaves it may be seen as dark red, sunken cankers.

Bacterial blight is chiefly seen in the Central and Eastern states. Water-soaked spots on the leaves become brown and brittle, killing the leaves; pustules appear on the pods and cankers on the stem, which may collapse. Mosaic causes light and dark mottling and corrugation of the leaves, stunting and crippling of the plant. This is a virus disease, serious in some years among the bean-growing areas of New York, and is spread by sucking insects such as aphids. Rust attacks the leaves, which turn from yellow to brown and then fall off, injuring the plant chiefly by defoliation. It occurs chiefly in some of the Middle Eastern states and California.

Lima beans are less subject to disease but may be attacked by bacterial spot at any part of the plant, including the pods, which show reddish-brown spots and later fall off. Downy mildew may produce a white growth over the pods in humid weather. The control recommended for both these diseases is spraying with Bordeaux mixture.

Insects

Ladybirds are beneficial insects in the garden, preying on aphids, but one of them, the Mexican bean beetle, which turned vegetarian, is a destructive, aggravating pest in the Eastern states, having spread from the Rocky Mountain area. It is coppery brown in color, with three rows of black spots on its back, and about a quarter inch long. Adults that have lived over the winter make their appearance while the plants are still young, and at once begin feeding and breeding. Soon thereafter clusters of tiny yellow eggs can be found on the underside of leaves, from which develop sluggish yellow larvae with destructive appetites.

If the bean rows are not too extensive, an effective control is to crush the egg clusters between finger and thumb, pick off the adults by hand, dropping them into a can holding some kerosene, and similarly destroy the larvae.

But dusting both sides of the leaves with an insecticide of .75 per cent rotenone content, particularly in the morning when the plants are damp with dew, gives very satisfactory results and leaves no harmful residues on the pods, as would the poisonous arsenicals. Some gardeners believe they get a better kill when the insecticide is applied as a spray; certainly this is at least equally effective. About two ounces of derris or cubé powder, 4 per cent rotenone content, should be stirred into three gallons of water. Pyrethrum preparations are also effective.

Other enemies—leaf hoppers, aphids, the seed-corn maggot, and the Japanese beetle—are mentioned in the chapter on insects.

OTHER BEANS

The Broad bean, *Vicia faba*, is one of the staple articles of diet in Europe and was long considered such in North America until it was displaced by the bush Lima. It is grown, however, in the eastern and western provinces of Canada and occasionally in the northeastern and northwestern areas of the United States. There are many varieties, the most popular of these being either of the Broad Windsor or the Long Pod class; the former is higher in quality, the latter in yield. Broad beans must be planted early, not only to escape the heat, but also to get well ahead in the cycle of growth before the arrival of the black aphis which invariably infests them. The most suitable soil is heavy but well drained, well limed, and well manured.

The Yard-long bean, *Vigna sesquipedalis,* is a pole member of the cowpea group which bears rather an exaggerated claim in its name, but pods of half a yard or more can easily be grown as a curiosity. They are of fairly good quality when young, and are dark green, round, and relatively small in diameter.

The Scarlet-runner bean, *Phaseolus multiflora,* is very rarely grown for food in North America, but if a climber is wanted as a background to the vegetable garden, it will form a handsome green screen over a trellis or fence, enlivened with spikes of scarlet blossoms to be followed by clusters of pods which, if picked when about four inches long, are very good. The seeds should be set two inches deep, six inches apart, and plants later thinned out to twelve inches or more. The soil must be well enriched.

BEET

Beta vulgaris

Two types of beet are grown in gardens: one for its enlarged root, known in other countries as beetroot, which is shortened in America to beet, by reason of its greater popularity; the other for its luxuriant leaves and broad stalks and known as Swiss chard or leaf beet. Mangel wurzel and sugar beet also belong to this species.

Beet is so easy to grow and so easy to cook that at least a short row of it is found in almost every garden, though it is not high in food value or vitamin content. Its sweetish flavor, tempered by a tang of the soil, is agreeable enough to most palates, especially as a constituent of salads; and even the gourmet who disdains it as mawkish will admit that it is indispensable in bortsch, one of the greatest of soups. Young beet tops are excellent as pot-herbs or greens.

Culture

While beet will grow in any average, properly drained garden soil, except perhaps during the hottest months of the South, it must grow quickly if the roots are to be tender and succulent. The soil should therefore be well prepared, so as to provide adequate moisture and plenty of plant food, by breaking up clods and pulverizing to a fine texture, adding old, well-rotted manure or compost, or commercial fertilizer. New manure must not be used just before planting beet as it is likely to encourage the tops at the expense of the roots, which may also suffer in shape and flavor. If old manure or compost is not available, work in a complete commercial fertilizer at the rate of about three pounds to one hundred feet of row. Preferably this should be strong in phosphorus, and in potash on muck soils.

Excessive acidity should be corrected, a mildly acid reaction of pH6 to pH7 being most suitable. Below

pH5.8 growth is increasingly affected, but in districts where potato scab is prevalent, commercial growers often refrain from liming, as the organism of this disease does not exist in acid soils.

Varieties

Practically all the beets grown in American gardens are now of the semi-globe type, though here and there the old Long Smooth Blood, with roots ten inches long, is still favored. It takes three months to develop, growing partly above the surface, and is a good variety for winter storage.

Probably the best early globular beet is Asgrow Wonder, requiring seven to eight weeks and preceding the well-known Detroit Dark Red (Improved Blood Turnip) by about ten days. Both of these are first class for either table use or canning, being of good shape and dark color.

A packet of seed will sow about thirty feet of row; an ounce, a hundred and fifty.

Planting

Beet may be sown as early as the ground can be made ready. For earlier roots seedlings may be started under cover and if a sowing is made in another row at the same time as transplanting, a succession will thus be arranged. Care should be taken at transplanting to see that the taproot is vertical and not bent around. Young beet plants are very tender, and it is important that their seedbed be especially well prepared—fine and smooth for three or four inches deep.

Eighteen inches apart is a satisfactory separation for the rows though they can be three or four inches nearer if space is limited. What is known as beet seed is really a small dried fruit containing from two to six seeds; therefore the planting rate is ten or twelve per foot. Where space is scarce and beets are popular, more roots per foot run may be grown if the plants stand zigzag in the row instead of being straight in line. In spring the depth should be about half an inch; in summer, for late beets, it may be as much as two inches in order to secure moisture, and the soil should be firmed over the seed. Short lengths of a row may be sown every two weeks.

Cultivation

Germination is somewhat slow because of the nature of the seed, and some gardeners sow a few radish seeds in the row as these will come up quickly and mark the line for cultivation, which should begin before the beets are up, so that the weeds do not get a foothold, though the hoe must not be allowed to damage the infant seedlings.

The seedlings may appear in little clumps, which should be thinned to one plant each. When these are four or five inches high, they are to be thinned again and the removed plants may either be used for delicate greens or transplanted elsewhere. At this thinning the distance apart the plants are left is determined by the size the gardener wishes to have his beets; some like them small, to be cooked whole, and therefore thin to two inches, but three to four inches is more usual.

Harvest

Beets may be enjoyed all through the season if successive sowings are made, and in late fall, when the first frost impends, they are pulled, the tops cut off—above the roots, to prevent bleeding—and cast on the compost heap. The roots are put into storage, where the best temperature is around 40° F.

LEAF BEET: SWISS CHARD

Originally only the leaves of beets were eaten, and among the ancient Greeks, notably a people of culture, were deemed worthy of a silver dish when ritually presented to Apollo in his temple at Delphi, whereas such lowlier vegetables as turnips rated only a platter of lead. Had they known it in its modern form, they would doubtless have dignified it with a golden dish, for this is now one of the best products of the garden. Its broad chards, or stalks, are served at table after the manner of asparagus and the leafy part as greens of pleasant flavor and texture. In addition, the plants are very resistant to heat and stand throughout the season; only outer leaves are removed at a cutting, and others grow to take their place.

Chard would be better known and more highly appreciated if it were more frequently on sale, but it is essentially a vegetable of the home garden, as it is ill-adapted to shipping in addition to the fact that the leaves are gathered singly and not the whole plant.

There are several varieties, one of which, with crumpled yellowish-green leaves and broad pale green chards, is named Lucullus, after a general of ancient Rome, who distinguished himself first in arms, later in luxurious hospitality. Dark Green has smooth leaves with narrower, light green chards, and Fordhook Giant has crinkled, dark green leaves with white chards.

Diseases and Insect Pests

The beets are relatively very free from enemies. In the East and Midwest leaf spot sometimes shows itself as gray dead spots ringed with purple, forming holes later. Such leaves should be burned. Potato scab occasionally roughens the roots; if it occurs, omit lime from next season's beet rows.

Blister beetles attack both types of beet leaves, reveling in chard, and the best control is to knock them off by hand into a can of kerosene and water. Flea beetles may be troublesome on young plants.

BROCCOLI

Brassica oleracea var. italica

Two very distinct members of the cabbage group are known as broccoli: one is the old-fashioned cauliflower broccoli, really a very late-maturing cauliflower, *Brassica oleracea* var. *botrytis,* now very rarely seen in home gardens, though grown commercially in the Northwest and California; the other, *Brassica oleracea* var. *italica,* described variously as Sprouting, Italian, or Calabrese broccoli, is one of the oldest of cultivated vegetables, long known in America but so infrequently grown in gardens that it is often referred to as new. It is now rapidly gaining in the popularity it well merits. Reference is made here only to green-sprouting broccoli. Other types, both purple and white, are known but not recommended for the home garden.

Sprouting broccoli first forms a dark green head, somewhat of the cauliflower type though smaller and looser, but of just as delectable quality at table; many would say still more. Even in the kitchen it is kind, for no disagreeable odor arises from its cooking, such as informs the whole household when cauliflower or cabbage is on the menu. After the head has been removed, numerous side shoots grow on the stalks and may be gathered from time to time to be used as was the central head.

Planting

Like cauliflower, sprouting broccoli is a plant of cool and moist conditions of growth. Seed is started indoors, about six weeks before the frost is expected to be out of the garden, and handled in the flats or frame just as cabbage or cauliflower would be. One packet will afford sufficient seed for even a large family garden; the number of plants to be raised will depend on individual preference and space.

Transplanting takes place as soon as possible to rows thirty inches apart or somewhat nearer, if space is limited, the plants being set two feet apart in the row. The head should be ready about sixty days later; the side shoots may be borne for the rest of the season but should be kept picked if they are to continue. In the North, a second planting may be made in August for autumn supplies. In the warm South, late planting is the rule.

The soil requirements, cultivation, diseases, and pests of sprouting broccoli are similar to those of cabbage and cauliflower, which see.

BRUSSELS SPROUTS

Brassica oleracea var. *gemmifera*

There are those who swear by Brussels sprouts and those who swear at them. The first are those who are partial to cabbage and kindred plants; the others are those whose tastes or digestions rebel and those disgruntled gardeners who have been disappointed in efforts to raise a crop.

One reason for lack of success is failure to appreciate the fact that this is a cool-weather vegetable, which takes about three months to mature. Where winters are warm and mild, sprouts may be had in spring, but in most parts of North America they should be regarded as proper to the year's end; they are, indeed, improved by a touch of frost. They may even be frozen on the stalk without much harm provided they are thawed gradually, but this should happen only once. Another reason is that, as sometimes occurs with species not in much demand, strains and seeds may vary considerably. It is therefore an elementary precaution to get seed of a named variety from a reputable source.

Culture

Brussels sprouts is a distinctive member of the cabbage tribe, with a long stalk or axis on which many buds or buttons—miniature cabbages an inch to two inches in diameter—are borne in the axils, or armpits, of the leaves.

For all practical purposes, Brussels sprouts are sown and grown as would be late cabbage. In estimating the number of plants to raise, it may be expected that each will produce a quart of sprouts if all goes well. If they are not likely to be a staple article of diet, but merely an occasional novelty, fifteen or twenty plants may seem a lot, but in England, where Brussels sprouts are paramount, fifty or sixty plants would be none too large a supply for a family of four or five and their guests. Anyhow, a packet of seed will suffice for the average garden.

The sprouts or buttons cannot all be picked at the same time; those at the bottom of the stalk grow first and are ready first. To encourage them and make picking easier, the lower leaves are gradually cut off, at about the height of the sprouts, when these are well grown, but the top or terminal leaves must always be left in place. If enough sprouts are growing when the real cold of winter comes, the whole plant may be lifted and placed in a cool cellar with a ball of earth about the roots.

CABBAGE

Brassica oleracea var. *capitata*

Few vegetable gardens in any part of the temperate areas of the world would be thought complete without a row of cabbage, even though it is one of the great market crops and usually in plentiful supply. It is not difficult to grow, it is useful in succession cropping, it is welcome in the kitchen, and it is one of the staple health foods, rich in vitamins, particularly B and C, and in minerals.

Certain basic factors are to be observed in preparing to grow cabbage. It is naturally a cool-weather plant, but is hardy and will tolerate considerable differences of temperature provided it has an adequate supply of moisture. Though it may perish in drought, it needs abundant sunshine, and it must have ample supplies of plant food, especially nitrogen and potassium. To these ends the soil for cabbage must be well worked into good tilth or mechanical condition and well enriched. Acidity is undesirable below $pH5.5$, when enough lime should be added to obtain a reaction of $pH6.0$ or 6.5.

Varieties

The many varieties of cabbage may be arranged in three groups: early, midseason, and late, of which the first is the most important, the second of much less interest to the home gardener, and the third for use only where there is ample space which can be given to the growing of large heads over a long season.

Among the early sorts, Jersey Wakefield, a little, pointed cabbage, long led the field but has now been largely superseded by Golden Acre, which is just as early—about two months from transplanting—and Copenhagen Market, both globe-shaped, very solid, and neat.

Glory of Enkhuizen is two to three weeks later and is generally considered the best of the midseason varieties. It is a handsome, large, round cabbage of very good quality.

Of the late cabbages, which take about four months from transplanting, there are two types: the round, best typified by Danish Ball Head or Hollander; and the flat, best known in the old Late Flat Dutch. These are both large heads, weighing about six pounds, solid, and more suitable for storage through the months of winter than the quicker-growing varieties.

Quite a distinct type of cabbage and much preferred

for its milder flavor by many people is the Savoy, with crumpled leaves, very dark green outside, lighter inside. Perfection Drumhead is the standard, Chieftain a newer strain.

Red cabbage is used for pickling; the best variety seems to be that known as Red Danish or Red Dutch.

Yellows-Resistant Varieties

In the Midwest, from Wisconsin south, and east to the Middle Atlantic states, young cabbage plants may become yellow, warped, and worthless within a month of being set out. This disease, known as cabbage yellows, is caused by a fusarium fungus, and where this organism infests the soil it is futile to plant cabbage of regular strains.

Resistant strains only should be planted in districts where the yellows disease is known to exist; these make it possible to raise cabbage, though perhaps the quality is not quite so good as in more favorable circumstances. Corresponding to Golden Acre is Resistant Golden Acre; to Glory of Enkhuizen there is Improved Globe, and to Hollander there is Wisconsin Hollander. A resistant pickling variety is Red Hollander.

Cabbage Plants

Garden cabbage is always raised from young plants, and quite an extensive industry for the supply of these to growers the country over is carried on in the South.

Local greenhouses also offer them for sale. The gardener who prefers to purchase his cabbage or other plants will do well to get them from a reliable source, to make sure of their being true to variety names and free from the germs of disease. But from a single packet of seed enough plants for even the larger garden can easily be grown in flats or frame, starting about six weeks before the garden is likely to be ready. The sand flat is very suitable for beginning cabbage, as it is desirable to have the plants develop good roots.

Six or eight seeds to the inch may be sown in the first flat, in rows two inches apart, and lightly covered. When the seedlings are two to three inches high they may be moved to the second flat, where they should be set about three inches apart each way. It is important that young cabbage plants be gradually and effectively hardened off.

Plants for winter cabbage are usually begun in an outside open seedbed in light, loose, not too rich soil. The date of sowing this will depend on the variety and the locality: in Northern gardens it might be in June, on the Gulf coast it might be in September. Anyhow, it should be so timed that the plants will reach full growth at the date when the first frost is expected. This will avoid bursting heads and instead should have them in good shape for storage. It may be advisable to spray or screen young plants to protect them from insect pests.

Cabbage is a biennial, accomplishing its life cycle in two seasons, in the second of which seed is normally developed. Occasionally, however, plants will throw up seed stalks in the first year, spoiling the head, which is a ball of incurved leaves. There is evidence to show that this premature bolting may be caused in part by growth in cold weather. Though the plant is hardy it had better not be subjected to much frost in its youth.

Transplanting

As noted above, cabbage needs plenty of plant food, especially nitrogen and potassium, but it is not too finicky about the formula as long as the soil is rich. The fertilizer should be worked in and the soil well pulverized and firmed down before transplanting begins.

The extent of the rows will of course depend not only on the number of plants to be grown but also on the variety. The small early Jersey Wakefield requires no more than about twelve inches in the row; average-sized varieties are set eighteen inches apart, with two feet or more between the rows; while the large late cabbages should have two feet between each plant in rows three feet apart. Only strong and vigorous plants should be set out, a little deeper than they stood in the frame and with the roots pointing down. The hole should be puddled, and after the plant has been placed in it it should be so filled and firmed that the rootlets are in full contact with soil. It is usually advisable to shade the young plants from strong sunshine in their first few days outside by paper protectors or berry boxes which, if they are being set out in early spring, can be turned over them on cold nights.

Some gardeners wrap a strip of paper around the stem to thwart the cutworms, though poison bait, as described in the chapter on insects, is better to clear them out of the area. Pieces of tar paper placed on the soil around the stem will prevent the cabbage maggot fly from laying its eggs there.

Cultivation

In the cabbage patch no weeds should be allowed to establish themselves among the young plants which later on will be spreading out some horizontal roots close below the surface and thus allowing for only shallow cultivation. Accordingly, the hoe or cultivator should be in action about once a week regularly though lightly until the plants are half grown, after which the shade of the plants will co-operate in stifling the weeds. Light cultivation in the early stages of growth has the additional advantage of making a soil mulch and thus tending to prevent evaporation of soil moisture; this is not so necessary when the roots are more fully developed.

Harvest

There is a knack in harvesting cabbage, and it is not merely cutting a head and bringing it indoors when one is wanted. The heads should be cut only when they are hard and solid, but, on the other hand, when they have reached that stage they should be deterred from further developing and bursting by giving the plant a twist or jerk to break some of the feeding roots and letting it stand in the row until the head is wanted.

For winter storage, plants should be free from injury or disease and are pulled up, roots and all, not cut, and kept in a cool cellar or storage room, preferably at a temperature just above freezing point. The cooler the storage, down to about 32°F., the longer the cabbage will keep, and the air should be rather dry to prevent development of storage rot.

In the North, cabbage is frequently stored in outdoor pits where the plants are laid in a row and the roots, but not the heads, covered with soil, with poles over the whole to carry a covering of dry leaves, straw, corn-stalks, and the like. Heads are cut as required without disturbing the stalks, which produce sprouts useful as spring greens. The cabbage keeps very well provided the temperature of the pit does not fall much below the freezing point. Or the plants may be stood on their heads in the lee of a sheltering wall and tree leaves, etc., heaped over them.

Diseases

Black rot is shown by yellow leaves and blackened veins; the head may rot and fall off. Blackleg not only blackens and rots the stem but also produces dark spots with minute black pimples on the leaves. The microscopic organisms of these and other diseases may be transmitted on seed which has been produced in infested areas, and where there is any possibility of this, good seedsmen disinfect the seed rather than take any chance of its being passed on. Cabbage and cauliflower seed, until recent years largely imported from Holland and Denmark, is now grown in coastal areas of the Northwest.

Cabbage yellows has been mentioned above. Clubroot is caused by one of the lowliest forms of life, a slime mold, which attacks the roots, causing large swellings on them. The plants take on a sickly yellowish look and are wilted in sunlight but perk up again in the evening when the disease is in the earlier stages. The slime mold flourishes only in acid soils, and if clubroot ever makes its appearance, hydrated lime should be applied to the proposed cabbage patch early in the following spring. Corrosive sublimate solution, one tablet to a pint of water or an ounce to ten gallons, around the roots of young plants in the row is also a deterrent both to clubroot and the cabbage maggot. NOTE: this is a deadly poison.

Insects

The harmless-looking white butterfly that flutters in the sun over the vegetable garden is the flying form of that destructive caterpillar, the cabbage worm, a sluggish, velvety-green creature an inch or more in length that eats holes in the leaves and even into the head. Dusting with rotenone or pyrethrum insecticides is effective and leaves no poisonous residue as would such arsenical poisons as Paris green, though this is still sometimes used until the cabbage heads begin to form. The cabbage looper, a thinner caterpillar which humps its back, may be similarly controlled. If cabbage aphids, gray waxy plant lice, are present, especially on young plants from which they suck the life juices, all of these pests may be cleared out by nicotine spray or dust.

In Northern gardens the cabbage maggot sometimes attacks the roots of young plants, burrowing into the stem and greatly weakening the plant. Corrosive sublimate solution, as mentioned above at clubroot, is applied shortly after the plants have been set out—half a cupful per plant poured onto the soil around the base of the stem.

This white maggot is the larva of a small fly resembling the housefly, which lays its eggs on or near the stem just below the soil surface. It is to defeat this intention that gardeners lay squares or discs of tar paper on the soil, fitted closely round the stem, when transplanting. The discs must, of course, be cut from center to circumference in order to get them around the stems. The inevitable cutworms were also mentioned above.

In the South, the harlequin, calico, or terrapin bug—a sucking insect, red with black spots, and about half an inch long—must usually be picked off, though rotenone sprays are said to be effective against the young bugs.

CHINESE CABBAGE: Pe-tsai

Brassica pekinensis

The Chinese have been farmers for forty centuries, and at some faraway time they produced this elegant vegetable, which bears only a very remote relation to the bucolic cabbage and resembles it merely in that its leaves are closely folded. It is more nearly related to the mustards, and would be better distinguished by the Chinese name Pe-tsai than by our appellations of Chinese cabbage or celery cabbage.

For a century past, possibly longer, Chinese cabbage has been grown by some few of the more eclectic American gardeners, but only in recent years has it become known to a wider circle, and its merits are now being more generally appreciated. The outer leaves may be used as potherbs or greens; the blanched heart furnishes a crisp, mildly flavored, and eminently digestible salad.

Varieties

Chihli, so named for the Chinese province of Chih-Li, now known as Hopei, is tall and columnar, standing about fifteen inches high with a diameter of about four inches. This is by far the most popular sort in American gardens.

Wong Bok is shorter and stouter, eight or nine inches

high by seven inches in diameter. It is grown to some extent in the South.

Quite a different though kindred species, often listed as a variety of Chinese cabbage, is Pak choi, *Brassica chinensis*. This does not form a solid head but grows more after the habit of Swiss chard. It is relatively un-known in American gardens. Both names, Pe-tsai and Pak choi, mean white vegetable; one is in the Mandarin dialect, the other in Cantonese.

The seed is small, and one packet will be enough in the average home garden for one sowing.

Preparation

Chinese cabbage is essentially a cool-weather plant and bolts to seed on the slightest provocation of summer heat. On the other hand, it is somewhat difficult to transplant successfully and therefore is better sown in the row in which it is to grow. In the relatively short time between sowing and summer the plant must grow quickly despite a rather poor root system. This it cannot do unless the soil is in good heart, damp but drained and well enriched, especially with nitrogen.

Sowing

The seeds are to be very sparsely sown, as soon as frost has gone, in rows two feet apart. The plants are after-ward thinned out when three inches high to stand about ten inches apart if of the Chihli variety, a little more if

Wong Bok. They may require some protection in the early stages. The fall crop should be timed for maturity before frost, allowing approximately seventy-five days for growth.

Cultivation

Weeds must not be allowed to interfere with the progress of this fast-growing plant and their removal with hoe or cultivator will help to create a dust mulch and conserve moisture.

Diseases and Insects

By comparison with cabbage or cauliflower, Pe-tsai is relatively free of enemies. In wet soil or wet seasons it is subject to a bacterial soft rot of the stem and possibly it might be attacked by clubroot. The cabbage butterfly does not appear to be attracted by it; stray aphids or other visitors yield to rotenone dust.

Harvest

Chinese cabbage may be kept in a cool cellar for several weeks. It is cut in the garden when the head is full and firm, and more often than not the outer dark leaves are discarded.

CARDOON

Cynara cardunculus

Pliny professed himself ashamed that the Romans of his day should spend $120,000 a year importing from

Libya and Spain these thistles which, he says, even the animals spurn. Nearly two thousand years later, the cardoon is still important in southern Europe and France, but in America it is a very minor crop and has rarely found a place in our gardens. Where there is space and inclination for such large plants, the artichoke, of which cardoon is the progenitor, is usually preferred. The two plants are much alike in habit of growth, but one is specialized in large flower heads, the other in massive leaf stalks or chards which are eaten either cooked or raw. Those who relish the somewhat bitter taste can also get chards, though not of such good quality, from artichoke.

Culture

In regard to soil requirements and growing conditions, cardoon does not differ from artichoke, but it is raised from seeds. French gardeners usually start these indoors, but they may very well be sown in the row as soon as the soil has begun to warm up. The best location in a home garden would be at the back or at one side, for these are large, bushy plants standing four or five feet high and will form a good background or screen. Three or four seeds are set in a group every two to three feet, later to be thinned out when three or four inches high to the strongest plant in each group. Cardoon must have sufficient moisture through the season or the stalks are likely to become pithy.

Blanching

To make the chards edible and white, the plants are blanched when, in late summer, they have attained full stature. Formerly the practice was to surround them with straw and earth them up, but a brown-paper wrapper is much cleaner and less laborious. On a day when the plants are dry, tidy them by removing any old leaves or debris that may have accumulated, then bring the stalks vertically together and tie them loosely. Around the plant tie the heavy brown paper to exclude light, and give the plant the support of a pole if this seems necessary. Throw up some soil around the base.

Harvest

About a month later the cardoons will be ready and may be used as required until the first frost comes, when the plants are moved to a storage cellar.

CARROT

Daucus carota

Carrots have been among the more popular vegetables of the garden ever since the Pastinaca Gallica, or French root, was brought to Rome in the early days of the Christian era. And of recent years it has acquired a new importance because of its high vitamin content, particularly vitamin A, which includes in its virtues that of enabling people to see better in the hours of darkness.

The plant is a biennial, apparently developed from the wild carrot, or Queen Anne's-lace, of the roadside. A century ago a well-known horticulturist, M. Vilmorin of Paris, by providing this bristly weed with rich soil succeeded at the fourth generation in changing its scraggy root to the size and flavor of the cultivated carrot. Others who endeavored to repeat this experiment have not been so successful.

Varieties

Though there are many varieties and more names, carrots for the garden fall into four groups: The small forcing or early outdoor type such as French Forcing, a little orange ball, or Amsterdam Forcing, which is of the lady-finger shape; the medium short, cone-shaped Chantenay, very useful for planting in heavier soils, Danvers Half Long, a popular variety originated in the past century near Danvers, Massachusetts, is similarly conical but longer; the cylindrical Nantes or Touchon, and the long, slender type now popular in the market, of which Imperator is the exemplar.

If only one variety is grown it might well be Nantes, so-called from its origination among the market gardeners of Nantes, a city of Brittany famous in history. This is a very neat, cylindrical type about six inches long, often served whole at table, and so nearly without a central core that it is frequently described as coreless. It is essentially a home garden variety, because absence of core means light tops and therefore unsuitability for the commercial grower, but its texture and flavor are admirable.

If the garden topsoil is deep and free from stones, Imperator may be grown. This comparatively recent development is somewhat of the Nantes type but about two inches longer and with stronger tops: a slim, attractive variety.

Carrot seed—really miniature dried fruit—is so small that a packet usually contains enough for upward of fifty feet of row.

Preparation

When a young carrot root is inching its way downward through the soil, it is not very well equipped to push a rock out of its way. Instead it will push around it, and the result is a crooked or forked carrot. Soil must therefore be well prepared, not merely by plain digging and raking but by double digging or trenching, removing stones, pulverizing clods, and making a fine, smooth bed deeper than the expected roots.

In general it is better not to plant carrots on newly broken soil unless it has been prepared with exceptional care. Even then, a short, stout variety should be sown, not a long, thin one.

Carrots are heavy feeders, and the soil should be liberally enriched, preferably with old, thoroughly rotted manure or well-made compost mixed not with the surface soil but with the second spit deep. Plenty of food makes for sweet and succulent roots, but on no account must new manure be used.

Sowing

The seed is sown in the row, which is first marked out with garden line and pegs, then a shallow drill is made by pressing the handle of a hoe along the line into the soil. As successive sowings should be made every two weeks in order to have young carrots always coming on, a proportionate amount of row is marked and the seed, mixed with sand for better distribution, is thinly strewn in it, then covered with a quarter inch of soil well firmed down. Rows are made fifteen to eighteen inches apart. Carrot seed is slow to germinate, and it is sometimes rec-

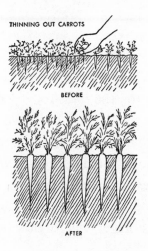

THINNING OUT CARROTS

BEFORE

AFTER

ommended that radish seed be mixed with it, to mark the line for cultivation.

The distance apart that plants will be left in the row depends on the diameter of the chosen variety and will be somewhere between two and four inches. Prior to this the row is likely to be thinned twice: first when the seedlings are well up and again three or four weeks later; at this second thinning there should be some young roots worth eating.

Cultivation

Since carrots grow slowly at first they must be helped by cultivation to keep the weeds from robbing them. Some of the rootlets extend horizontally and not far below the surface, therefore cultivation should be rather shallow. This will be quite effective, however, if done regularly and before the weeds have time to establish themselves.

Harvest

Carrots should be pulled while still young, at the first sign of yellowing on the tops, for if left too long in the soil they will get tough and not be worth eating. When the first frost is due, carrots of the last sowing should be loosened with a fork, lifted, topped to within half an inch of the shoulder, exposed to sunlight for a few hours so as to destroy any soil bacteria of the rot-causing type, and placed in cool storage, where they may be kept for several months if the air does not become dry and the temperature can be kept, for preference, just above the freezing point. The roots are often laid in sand or straw.

Diseases

Bacterial soft rot sometimes attacks carrots that have been injured by other organisms or animals, especially in wet conditions, or when the roots are stored without proper ventilation and at temperatures too high or too low. There is no remedy; prevention is the only safeguard.

Leaf blight occasionally kills leaves in wet seasons. Spraying with Bordeaux mixture or copper-lime dust will control the infection.

Insect Pests

Carrots are just as fortunate in regard to infrequency of insect enemies as of diseases, but where the carrot rust fly spreads it can do much damage. This little dark green fly lays its eggs in the soil near carrot, celery, or parsnip plants. When the larvae develop, they go down to the tip of the root and begin feeding, working up and making rusty tunnels through the root.

There are two broods in summer, at three-months' intervals, and in New York it was found that carrots sown in June escaped the first brood and were harvested before the second. A pound of naphthalene flakes distributed over a hundred feet of row gave complete control.

CAULIFLOWER

Brassica oleracea var. *botrytis*

This epicurean vegetable is esteemed by many connoisseurs the best of all the cabbage tribe, and certainly few of his products redound more to the credit of the gardener than a well-formed, shapely, firm, but tender head of white cauliflower.

Its chief difference from cabbage lies in the fact that it is cultivated for its dense and thickened flower cluster instead of a mass of folded leaves, but in a general sense the cultural requirements of cabbage and cauliflower are alike. The latter is, however, a more tender plant and cannot endure frost as would cabbage, collard, kale, or Brussels sprouts, nor will it head satisfactorily in the high heat of summer; accordingly, it is grown in spring and fall.

Varieties

The varieties in general use are Early Snowball and Dwarf Erfurt; a somewhat later-maturing variety known as Dry Weather or Danish Giant is often planted for the fall crop or where conditions are not too favorable for cauliflower culture. The old so-called cauliflower-broccoli types, previously mentioned under broccoli, are not suitable for the home garden.

Culture

The ideal soil for cauliflower is very fertile and moist but well drained. Good preparation and enrichment are therefore necessary, and especially on sandy soils humus will be incorporated to good advantage.

Plants started in flats or frames, just as for cabbage, are invariably used, and whether the gardener raises these himself or buys them, he should be careful that the source of supply is entirely reliable, as there is considerable variation in the worth of some strains of cauliflower.

Spring plants are set out as soon as frost has definitely gone, and fall plants between two and three months before it is expected to return. The distance between plants should be two feet, with two and a half to three feet between the rows. Twenty-five plants will probably be enough for a family of four or five.

Weeds must be kept down, and as soon as the heads begin to form the outer leaves should be tied loosely over the center to afford protection from the sun. The tie should not be so tight as to exclude ventilation, which might lead to rot. Commercial growers often use cords of different colors to show which heads were tied first, but this is hardly necessary in the home garden unless a large number of plants is grown.

When the heads are firm and full they should be cut and not allowed to stand on the plants lest they become discolored and loose. The outer leaves are trimmed to the upper level of the head before presenting these trophies to the kitchen.

The diseases and insect pests which may afflict cauliflower are those of cabbage also, and have been described under that head.

CELERIAC

Apium graveolens var. *rapaceum*

This type of celery does not produce edible stalks but instead a bulbous base of about three inches' diameter, very useful in the concoction of celery soup or celery sauce, and indeed may be dignified with the precedence of a vegetable in its own right, rather than a mere substitute for the better-known celery, when served in the manner of kohlrabi or turnip, or sliced thinly into the salad bowl.

Culture

The seedlings are to be raised with the same care as celery and similarly transplanted to fine, rich soil, but set rather shallow and at four or five inches apart. Then, and all through the growing season, they must have sufficient water. When the knob has formed, the soil is to be drawn down and side roots cut off, a few at a time. When maturity is approaching, the soil is to be drawn up again over the knob, which will have some blanching effect.

For winter reserve supplies, remove all leaves except a

couple in the center, so that the plant will not exhaust the knob by throwing up others, and store in the root cellar or cover by ridging and topping with leaves and straw if left in the row.

CELERY

Apium graveolens

Celery is such a fastidious plant and demands so much from the garden that, under ordinary circumstances, its production is better left to specialized commercial growers. In the average home garden, the money, time, and trouble that must be invested in celery will yield bigger dividends if applied to other vegetables.

Briefly, the conditions for celery growing are a light soil full of humus and fertilizer, continuous moisture, and the persistent attention of the gardener.

Preparation

The soil cannot be too well prepared for celery; it must be deeply worked, made thoroughly mellow, and liberally endowed with humus—preferably in the form of old manure—supplemented with commercial fertilizer of such analysis as 5-10-5 at the rate of about a pound to each fifty square feet.

The reason for this thorough preparation is that the root system of celery is like a bunch of hairs, ill-adapted for foraging round to supply it with the large amounts of moisture and inorganic plant food it requires. The deep digging and the humus help to conserve moisture; the concentration of manure and fertilizer provides the needed supplies of food. Some growers give a top-dressing of nitrate of soda at the rate of a pound to sixty feet of row just before blanching begins.

If the garden should be in a muck soil area, the humus is already there. Most of the celery that comes to market is grown on muck soil, and there the growers use fertilizer of high potash content, such as 3-12-18.

Two plantings of celery are usually made, one for spring celery, one for winter, and the rows of these are marked out differently. For early celery, the so-called self-blanching varieties are used, but they are only self-blanching if set close together, as at six inches apart in the row, with the rows a foot apart. The preparation for this old method is a bed about four feet wide, as mellow and fine as it can be made.

Alternatively, the rows for early celery should be at least two feet apart; for winter celery four feet. It is to be observed, however, that a bed from which the sunlight is so effectively excluded as to blanch the stalks is likely to be a good place in hot and humid weather for the propagation of germs causing rot.

Varieties

The term "self-blanching" is applied to most of the early varieties, but no celery will be entirely blanched without some assistance in the exclusion of light. Golden Plume, which was developed from Golden Self-Blanching, is probably the best all-round early variety; and Utah, which is of the standard Pascal type, but takes a week less to mature, is recommended for the late crop.

A packet of seed should produce at least five hundred plants.

Sowing

Celery seed is so small and so tedious to get started properly that seedling plants are worth what little they cost, provided they are of the desired variety, are well developed, and free from the germs of disease—which is to say they should be bought only from a competent and reliable source.

Otherwise, about ten weeks before the garden is likely to be ready, the tiny seeds may be scattered thinly on the surface of a sand-and-water flat, dusted over with a trifle of sand, and covered with a cloth, which will save them from disturbance and retain moisture. Three or four weeks later the sprouts appear, the cloth is removed, but the flat, which must always be damp, is kept covered with glass, slightly raised for ventilation. When the seedlings stand an inch high they are to be pricked out into a second flat and set two inches apart each way. They must be hardened off very gradually and with great care, for they are fragile and unfit to stand any shocks. When four or five inches high they are ready for transplanting.

For the late crop seed may be sown outdoors, when soil and air are warm, in a fine, well-made seedbed. Mix the seed with sand to facilitate distribution and sprinkle it in rows about eight inches apart. Cover with a dusting of sand or soil and a piece of burlap which must always be kept damp. Thin out when ready, setting the thinned seedlings in other rows.

Transplanting

When the seedlings are moved to the bed or row, the soil must be damp and the temperature similar to what they have been accustomed to. A shallow trench three or four inches deep is made and holes six inches apart made with the dibber or transplanting trowel; the plants must be carefully set in, the soil firmed around them, with no chance of an air pocket below, and the whole watered. Water daily until the plants are well established. The little trench will be gradually filled in. If the plants are six inches apart, a thirty-foot row obviously contains sixty plants, which is a good supply of early celery, though not too much of the late, for the average family.

Cultivation

Weeds positively must not be allowed to make any progress in the celery bed or rows; yet with the fine and fibrous roots of celery, cultivation must be shallow, which means that it must be fairly frequent until the plants develop sufficiently to shade the soil for themselves. Nor must the soil ever be allowed to become dry, for drought is fatal to celery.

Blanching

Celery must be blanched, or bleached, to remove its naturally bitter taste and make it edible, to improve its appearance, and to encourage development of the central stalks. Commercial growers use boards set on edge along the rows close to the stalks and held apart at the top by cleats or hooks. Another method is to use long bands of waterproof paper held in position by upright metal rods.

For the home gardener there are convenient paper sleeves, or tubes, one of which may be slipped over a plant so as to enclose the stalks and leave the foliage projecting over the top. Or the stalks of each plant may be wrapped in a broad strip of heavy paper, tied in position with raffia tape or soft twine. By bleaching the plants in successive groups, the early celery will become available gradually instead of all at once.

The old method of earthing up is not applied to the early crop as it may encourage rot, but for the late crop in areas subject to freezing it affords protection, and the plants may be kept in the ridges a considerable part of the winter if a deep layer of straw, leaves, and litter is spread over the tops. The plants should be lightly tied together first, in order to keep dirt out of the hearts.

The time required for blanching depends upon season

and circumstances, probably averaging two weeks in summer and twice as long in late fall.

Harvest

The best way to lift celery is to drive a sharp spade just below the plant and cut the roots. In warm weather it should not be allowed to wilt through lying around but should be trimmed, washed, and put in the icebox until required for use.

Late celery can be very successfully continued indoors if taken up with the roots and replanted in a cool cellar. The plants should be cut from the row with a long knife, circling around the base so as to form an inverted cone of roots and soil, and replanted at once in the cellar with the same soil level, so that the stalks will not become wet. Plenty of moisture must be supplied, but only to the roots, in the first couple of weeks and afterward as necessary to keep the soil damp. A box over the plants will keep them blanched if the cellar is light.

Diseases

Blights which cause spots or dead areas on the plants may attack celery if it has been planted in the same place for a number of seasons, or if old celery trimmings and trash have been left lying around in the neighborhood. The remedy is weekly spraying with Bordeaux mixture or dusting with copper-lime dust.

Old celery fields in the commercial growing areas

around the Great Lakes and in California may contain fusarium fungi, which make plants yellowish, stunted, and bitter. This disease is the yellows and is combated by planting resistant varieties such as Michigan Golden. The green varieties appear to be exempt from attack.

In the South, celery is among the vegetables which suffer from rootknot following the attacks of nematodes.

Insects

A small caterpillar with pale green lengthwise stripes may make a web joining several leaves. It is the celery leaf tier, also found on other plants, eating the undersides of leaves, and may be controlled by pyrethrum or rotenone dust.

The celery worm is about two inches long, bright green with plain and fancy bars crosswise. This is the larva of the large black swallowtail butterfly and rarely does much damage. It may be picked off by hand. The tarnished plant bug is found all over the country, damaging many herbaceous plants by sucking sap from leaves and shoots. The adult is a brownish oval bug, about one fifth of an inch long, with lighter mottlings that produce the tarnished effect. What celery growers call black joint is caused by its punctures and feeding. Spraying once a week with sulphur and slaked lime, eight ounces of each to a gallon of water, is the recommended control if there is any considerable invasion of this pest.

CHAYOTE

Sechium edule

The name of this fruitful vine, being a modification of the Aztec chayotli, bespeaks its American antiquity, and its many synonyms of limited territorial application—as chuchu, huisquil, mirliton, pipinella, vegetable pear, and mango squash—may indicate that the plant was growing over a wide area before the arrival of European settlers.

Chayote is a perennial, and grown as such in the warmer parts of the South, but is sensitive to frost and if tried in any cooler area had better be regarded as an annual of long growing season. The vine is a climber, of the cucumber or melon type; the fruits are more or less pear-shaped around a single large flat seed but vary greatly on different plants in size, shape, color, and quality; from pale green to dark green, from a few ounces to two pounds, and from fibrous to fiberless flesh. They may be boiled or baked and used in many ways, with meats or in puddings, fritters, etc. The tuberous roots are edible and in tropical conditions produce smaller ones which are used like potatoes. The young shoots are also eaten, and the vine foliage is agreeable to cattle.

Culture

The entire fruit is usually planted on its side and with the point slightly exposed, where the vine is to grow, but shoots from the base of a good plant are often preferred, as seeds do not always reproduce true to type. Such a large and vigorous grower requires rich soil as well as a trellis or other support to climb upon, where it will quickly provide attractive decoration and, if it is a good type in favorable conditions, fifty to a hundred or more fruits. These may be expected in October and November, from spring planting, and, if the vine survives, a few more fruits may appear in the following May.

Diseases and Insect Pests

Rootknot is troublesome where the nematodes infest the soil, and this often leads to annual planting. The cucumber beetles, pickle worm, and other insect pests of allied plants may also attack the chayote.

CHICORY

Cichorium intybus

One of the easiest vegetables to grow and one of the most rewarding through the following winter is the chicory known as witloof, which is to say white leaf. The word is Flemish, for it was among the market gardeners near Brussels that the method of forcing was developed which produces the neat white chicons known, with double incorrectness, as French endive.

Variety

There is but one variety, witloof, which is a strain of the Magdeburg large-rooted chicory used extensively in Europe, and in some parts of America, to flavor coffee. These are cultivated forms of the wild chicory which graces our roadsides and many a waste place, described by Emerson as

> *Grass with green flag half-mast high,*
> *Succory to match the sky.*

Culture

Nothing could be simpler than the garden culture of chicory. Work the soil well, as for any heavy-rooted crop, and fertilize it to encourage strong growth. Sow the seed thinly in the row, cover it lightly, and firm it down. Restrain the weeds until the chicory is big enough to smother them. Thin the plants to six inches apart when three or four inches high, using the thinnings either to extend the row or to be boiled for greens. The length of the row will be a matter of the family appetite for this delicacy. Twenty-five feet and one packet of seed might be the allowance on the average.

Harvest and Storage

This trouble-free vegetable stands throughout the summer, its large leaves sending down food supplies to be stored in the parsniplike roots. The gardener's real work on it begins in the late fall. The tops are cut off within an inch of the crown, the roots are lifted with a fork, and any long, thin tips trimmed down. Most of the roots will be stored in an outside shed; half a dozen may be taken into the house cellar. If they are stood upright in damp sand or soil and covered with inverted pots or boxes so as to exclude all light, they will send up in three or four weeks the compact, blanched heads about five inches long which merely require to be cut and dressed to provide one of the best of winter salads. As a head is removed, the root is replaced by another one from the shed or, more probably, several at a time have attention.

Another procedure in the cellar is to lay down first a layer of soil, sand, or peat moss, about two inches deep; on this put a horizontal layer of roots with their tails to the wall and their heads in front, then an inch or two of soil, etc., then another layer of roots a little farther back toward the wall, and so on, to a depth of perhaps two feet. The pile is to be regularly sprinkled to keep it moist and covered with whatever is available to exclude light. In due course shoots will protrude, not straight and compact as in the witloof heads, but loose and bent upward. The largest of these are cut at any time when required without disturbing the roots and form what is known as Barbe de Capucin, a term used in France for at least two centuries and suggesting that the friars of that austere order were well known in everyday life then.

An unorthodox method of producing witloof heads—

but one which may be practiced unless and until cold penetrates and puts a stop to growth—is to leave the roots in the row after they have been topped, cover them with a six- or eight-inch layer of hay, and ridge up with soil. A layer of fresh manure over all will help to defy the cold still longer.

COLLARD

Brassica oleracea var. *acephala*

Collard is colewort; cole is from the Latin *caulis*, stalk; wort is an Anglo-Saxon word meaning plant, so the collards are the stalk plants, thus named by Pliny in the first century of our era to distinguish them from other greens. To this day the cabbage tribe as a whole is often referred to under the generic term of coles or cole plants, corresponding to the French *chou* and the German *kohl*. The plural word collards is a reminder that any of the tribe, up to a certain point of growth, can be used for greens of the cabbage type, and indeed many of the various young plants are so used, but the sturdy, non-heading cabbage deserves a name in its own right and is now the collard.

It is a plant of major importance in the South, where, by its hardy constitution, it withstands the summer heat and winter cold and is highly esteemed for flavor as well as for its easy cultivation.

Varieties

The standard variety is Georgia or Southern collard, some thirty or more inches in height and bearing a loose cluster of large cabbage-like leaves which may be picked a few at a time as required and before they mature so much as to be tough.

Culture

In general, the culture of collard and that of cabbage are similar, but in the South collard may be sown in the garden row, where the plants are thinned to stand about two feet apart, with three feet between the rows. Sowing is usually in both spring and fall. In the North, plants should be set in summer for late greens, which will be improved by the first frosts.

Cultivation must be carried on, and as the plants are gradually stripped of their lower leaves they may need the assistance of a stake to support the top cluster. The diseases and insects which attack cabbage may be expected on collard also and may be similarly controlled.

SWEET CORN

Zea mays var. saccharata

Maize has been cultivated in America from time immemorial and was so exclusively the staple grain crop when the early English travelers arrived that they called it Indian wheat or Indian corn. But the antiquity of *sweet* corn is uncertain and though grown by many tribes it was apparently not of great importance in the Indian way of life. Only in the past century have varieties of sweet corn come to be differentiated by name and to take a considerable place in American gardens. The slowness of its start, however, has been compensated by the progress made in recent years through the application of modern methods of plant breeding and the consequent development of hybrid varieties more vigorous, higher yielding, more resistant to disease, and often adapted to the growing conditions of particular localities.

Corn is naturally open-pollinated, that is to say, the pollen discharged from the male elements in the tassels is air-borne until it chances to alight on receptive silks. In hybrid corn breeding, on the other hand, pollination is controlled, so as to take advantage of the phenomenon of hybrid vigor. This is seen in unusually fine offspring resulting from the crossing of inbred plants; namely, those which have come from the fertilization of each of their ancestors with its own pollen for some generations.

Thus, for example, a corn breeder may select a plant which shows resistance to disease when others around it are infected. Next season all the kernels it produced are sown, and when each plant grows its tassels are enclosed in tied bags so that the pollen they shed will be collected. The immature silks are similarly enclosed to seclude them from any pollen but that of their own plant, which is applied when the tassel bag is swiftly substituted for the one that has been covering them.

All the plants in the row are similarly selfed, as it is called, and all are inoculated with the germs of the disease by means of a syringe. Some may continue to show resistance, and the best of these are selected for further inbreeding and testing during the following season.

As the inbreeding progresses, succeeding generations have less and less vitality but always preserve that factor of disease resistance until the plant breeder is satisfied that this is definitely fixed in his inbreds, so that if they grow at all they will be immune to the disease. They have become entirely uniform, so that one plant looks, and is, exactly like another—and usually they are all miserable-looking little runts.

At the same time another inbred line of different parentage may have been similarly produced for, say, narrow kernels. When the pollen of one line is transferred to the silks of the other, the two desired characters should be perpetuated in the seed then developed, and when this seed is planted, hybrid vigor is demonstrated. As if Nature were trying to make up for the imposition of inbreeding, the hybrid plants are strong and lively, in complete contrast to their undersized parent inbreds, but they retain the characteristics of uniformity, resistance to disease, and narrow kernels.

The story does not end there, however, for if seed from the hybrids be saved and planted, the following generation will show an apparent effort by Nature to undo the work of the plant breeder: hybrid vigor is lost, there will be no uniformity, and the acquired characters begin to be dispersed. The inbred lines are therefore perpetuated year after year with great care by the corn breeder, and a number of their plants are crossed by controlled pollination to produce the hybrid seed which is sold for planting.

Varieties

For wide adaptability to the growing conditions of different areas combined with yield and quality, Golden Cross is at present the best sweet-corn hybrid. It is a strong-growing midseason type, resistant to wilt, with large yellow ears of excellent eating quality.

Spancross and Marcross are earlier and smaller yellow varieties; Stowell's Evergreen Hybrid is a later, larger white; but the gardener will do well to consult the list of hybrids recommended for use by his state agricultural experiment station.

Among the open-pollinated varieties Golden Bantam is still a favorite but it is a small ear and the plant is very susceptible to wilt. Black Mexican, which is white at the eating stage, is said to be the sweetest of all. Country Gentleman, a white variety with shoe-peg kernels closely set and not in rows, retains some of its long-standing popularity. But there are scores of others.

For the warmer South, outside the regular sweet-corn-growing area, Honey June, a late white variety, is especially adapted, and its long husks afford good protection against the ear worm, which is very prevalent there. Older, semi-sweet, so-called roasting ears used in the South are, in order of maturity, Hastings' Early Market, Truckers' Favorite, and Adams' Large Improved.

Seed is sold in four-ounce packets, each enough for about a hundred feet of row or fifty to sixty hills. Most gardeners who have sufficient space plant an early and a midseason variety.

Preparation

In marking off the plot for corn it is well to remember that the formation of kernels depends on efficient pollination, and, as the pollen is diffused by air rather than carried to specific places by insects, a long single row is less likely to be well pollinated than several short rows in a block, or a number of hills.

Four rows of twenty-five feet are therefore better than one long row of a hundred feet, and the corn may alternatively be set in hills, or groups, of three plants each, with three feet between hills. The rows are neat, but the hills make weeding easier.

Corn needs fertile soil, well drained but retentive of moisture, and if any old rotted manure or compost is available, the corn plot is therefore a good place to use it. Or a complete fertilizer of such analysis as 5-10-5, on average loam soil, may be worked in at the rate of about seven pounds to a hundred feet of row. This preparation should be done as soon as the frost is well out of the ground, a week or two before the seed is sown. Some gardeners prefer to apply fertilizer in a narrow strip on either side of the row, about three inches away from the seed, so that the fertilizer may not come in contact with seed.

Sowing

Seed is sown in the garden, though to get earlier ears a few seedlings may be raised indoors in bands or pots, starting a month before planting time. If planting in rows, make these thirty inches apart, setting the seeds three or four to a foot, later to be thinned out so that the plants stand nine to twelve inches apart, depending on the variety. One inch is usually deep enough to set the seeds in spring. Hills should be three feet apart each way for the large midseason or late varieties, thirty inches for the smaller early sorts. Set five or six seeds for each hill, later to be thinned to three plants. Corn should be eaten at the prime picking stage, and successive plantings are made every week or ten days to this end. The number of plantings and the amount planted each time will depend on local conditions and individual preference, but the first one will be when the soil is warm and the last one three months before the average first frost date. For the last plantings some of the early-maturing seed is used. Of course the ears will not be ready with the same regularity as the intervals of planting, because they grow more quickly in warmer weather, and a difference of two weeks in sowing will probably be reduced to a week in harvesting.

Cultivation

Shallow and persistent cultivation is to be practiced until the plants are about half their full growth, to keep down the weeds and, even if there were no weeds, to conserve moisture. Deep cultivation will at any time tend to cause loss of soil moisture by evaporation and should not be necessary if the seedbed has been well prepared; it is also likely to cut roots when these have grown. As the plants develop, secondary or prop roots grow a little above the surface; soil should be drawn up to these in course of cultivation, and in this way the hills are formed. Secondary side shoots, known as tillers or suckers, often arise from the base of the stalk, but they need not be removed, as experiments have indicated that they do not adversely affect the growth or yield of the plants.

Harvest

The ear should be plump and well filled, the silks shriveled and brown, but ears should not be allowed to stand on the stalk after the kernels have filled out. A strip of husk may be turned back to make sure that the ear is ready, and replaced if it is not. The precise time to pick corn is the moment the water is boiling in the pot, so that sweetness may be fully maintained, but little is lost if ears are kept in an icebox for a couple of hours. The only way in which fresh, edible ears can be kept in storage is by quick freezing, but corn is excellently preserved by canning, on or off the cob, or in succotash.

Diseases

The major disease of sweet corn is bacterial wilt, which causes shriveling and death of plants, especially in hot weather and when nearly full grown. If the lower stalk of an affected plant is cut across and squeezed, a yellow ooze is indicative of the work of the bacteria, which may have been transmitted by flea beetles or cucumber beetles or in seed from infected plants. There is no cure, but all stalks suspected of infection should be burned to prevent spread of the disease. Prevention is better: plant only resistant varieties.

Corn smut appears in late summer as pallid, shining growths on ears or tassels, which grow rapidly and eventually burst, discharging a powdery black mass of spores. Infected parts of the plants should be destroyed before this happens. The growths are said to be edible when young.

Insect Pests

The corn ear worm is so called because it does more damage to corn than other crops, but it is also the tomato fruit worm, the cotton bollworm, and it attacks many other vegetables. It grows to about two inches long, is green to purplish brown in longitudinal stripes and markings. The eggs are laid on young silks by the adult moth; when the larvae emerge they work down into the tips, which they damage not only by feeding but also because the openings they make may lead to decay. Clipping the silks, applying oil impregnated with pyrethrum or dichlorethyl or dusting them with insecticides and other remedies have been tried with more or less success, but in the South, where this pest is particularly prevalent, the only really effective control is very long husks projecting beyond the ear tip as in the variety Honey June.

In the North, the European corn borer, the larva of a night-flying moth which lays its eggs on the leaves, burrows into the stalks and ears anywhere, and is often first detected in a plot when some of the tassels break and fall over. The usual control is the slow one of eliminating it from the neighborhood by disposing of all corn plants and garden trash so that larvae cannot live over to another year, but effective insecticidal sprays have recently been developed, and dusting the axils of the leaves with rotenone once a week and after rain has been recommended. The white scale-like egg masses on the underside of leaves should also be dusted if seen. Damage may also be done by the Southern corn rootworm—which is the twelve-spotted cucumber beetle at an early stage—wireworms, and other general pests.

CORN SALAD

Valerianella olitoria

An insipid salad herb, as nearly tasteless as a plant can be, but very easily grown in early spring or late fall. It is sown in the row, requires no attention beyond thinning to about six inches apart and watering if the soil becomes dry. A rosette of spoonlike, gray-green leaves is formed in about two months, and as many as desired may be picked at a time.

CRESS

Lepidium sativum

Sometimes known as pepper-grass. A quick-germinating, quick-growing plant with finely curled bright green leaves, daintier in appearance than mustard and a little sharper in its pleasantly pungent flavor, which is not nearly so robust as that of water cress. Sow two or three feet at a time in the open row at the first working of the garden and repeat weekly. Snip the tops off when the plants are about four inches high, leaving the stalks about an inch above ground, and a second growth will develop. Dust with rotenone or pyrethrum nonpoisonous insecticide if flea beetles exhibit their partiality for cress.

UPLAND CRESS, apparently so named to distinguish it from water cress, which it resembles in flavor, is *Barbarea verna*, an easily grown herb of the mustard family which should be better known by those who are partial to such pungency. It is usually sown in early fall for its glossy green leaves, deeply incut on either side, used in winter salads. It is also called winter cress and, in the South, scurvy-grass, a name which properly belongs to *Cochlearia officinalis*, also of the mustard family, with heart-shaped leaves and tarry flavor.

WATER CRESS, *Roripa nasturtium-aquaticum*, can hardly be accounted a garden plant as its natural habitat is in gentle streams. It can be grown from cuttings or seed in sand or soil kept continually wet, but any temptation to put it into a garden pool should be resisted, as it will choke up the pool. It is at its best in cool and cold weather, becoming altogether too strongly flavored in the warmth of summer.

CUCUMBER

Cucumis sativus

Cucumber vines sprawl over so much territory that they are not admissible to the small garden, and even where plenty of room is available it is well to weigh the ease with which cucumbers can be obtained at market against the trouble of growing them. They are not of that choice company of vegetables which should be eaten as soon as picked; their food value is low and some people find them quite indigestible; the plants are tender and difficult to keep in healthy condition through the season; the pestiferous cucumber beetles and bugs will seek them out from afar and can play hide-and-seek with the gardener around such large plants. On the other hand, from the commercial grower's point of view the fruits are convenient for shipping and the market demand is good; therefore technical equipment overcomes many of the difficulties and large supplies are raised in mass production.

Preparation

The usual method of growing cucumbers is in hills about five feet apart each way in each of which a forkful of old manure is buried. According to an old rhyme eight seeds should be planted

One for the beetle, one for the crow,
Two for the cutworm, four to grow.

But six seeds should be enough and the best three plants from these left to grow. Some experienced growers, however, prefer to sow cucumbers and similar vines in a row and keep thinning out the plants as they grow on the theory that a high population of plants is the best insurance against insects and disease.

Cucumber is a warm-weather crop and the sowing is not done until danger of frost is past. Because transplanting is difficult, seeds are rarely sown indoors but may be started on a piece of upturned sod or in bottomless bands.

Four or five hills should afford enough cucumbers for a family of as many people.

Varieties

Cucumbers are grown either for slicing or for pickling, and whatever aspersions are cast on the digestibility of slicing cucumbers, no one will deny that the small fruits make excellent pickles.

A long, dark green type is now the vogue for slicing and is best represented by Colorado, eight to nine inches long and with relatively few spines; A & C of similar length; and Straight-8 which, as indicated by its name, averages eight inches. Of the pickling cucumbers National Association is the most widely used. Gherkins, *Cucumis anguria*, which are not true cucumbers, are sometimes planted for very small pickles, especially in the South. One packet of any variety should be sufficient.

Culture

The young plants may need protection from beetles by day and cold by night until the vines begin to run. For this purpose two half hoops set at right angles and covered with cheesecloth, which must be closed at the bottom, are very effective. Keep cultivating until the foliage is developed; avoid stepping on the vines, which may kill the growing end. Spraying with fungicides and insecticides will doubtless be necessary.

Harvest

Fruits in different stages of maturity are borne on each vine; all those that are ready should be picked daily so that the others may develop better and the growing season be prolonged; picking should be done only when the leaves are dry, to lessen the possibility of spreading disease. Small cucumbers for pickling will be gathered as and when desired.

Diseases

Bacterial wilt, which may shrivel plants and fruits alike, is spread by cucumber beetles, in the digestive tract of which the bacteria spend the winter.

Mosaic, otherwise known as white pickle, shows in yellow and green mottling of the leaves with warted, warped, and blotched fruits. This is a virus disease spread by insects or by other means, possibly first from weedy host plants in the neighborhood, then from plant to plant in the garden. Anthracnose and downy mildew are fungous diseases which cause spots on the leaves and spoil many fruits. Spraying with Bordeaux mixture is recommended.

In the South, cucumbers, in common with other plants, suffer from rootknot, caused by nematodes.

Insect Pests

The striped cucumber beetle, about a quarter inch long, with yellow and black longitudinal stripes, and the twelve-spotted cucumber beetle, a little larger, not only devour leaves and other parts but spread serious diseases. They may be controlled with rotenone or other insecticidal dust. If dusting is started as soon as the seedlings appear and continued at regular intervals until the plants are well established, damage by cutworms and beetles can be kept at a minimum.

Squash bugs, vine borers, and melon aphids also attack cucumbers.

DANDELION

Taraxacum officinale

Those who like a slightly bitter taste in salad herbs and are less acquainted with the virtues than the vices of dandelion should make trial of its fresh young leaves in spring. The cultivated varieties have larger, more succulent leaves, which are sometimes blanched to delete some of the bitter quality, when they are used either for salad or as greens. The roots may also be forced in the cellar to produce a sort of Barbe de Capucin similar to that obtained from chicory. Improved Thick-Leaved is the usual variety. It is sown in the row and the plants are thinned to stand a foot apart. Needless to say, it is of easy culture and will take care of itself anywhere, but it will produce better leaves in good soil. The roots left in the ground over winter will afford early greens in the following spring.

DASHEEN : TARO

Colocasia esculenta

This close relation of the elephant's ear, familiar in the flower garden and resembling it in appearance, is grown as a long-season crop in the South Atlantic and Gulf coast states for its tubers or cormels—which are also known as taro root, a widely used food of the tropics—and its forced, succulent shoots.

Trinidad is about the best of many varieties; tubers of three or four ounces are planted three inches deep, two feet apart in the row. This is a highly nutritious vegetable of nutty flavor, used in much the same way as potatoes or sweet potatoes.

EGGPLANT

Solanum melongena

From France to Turkey and in the lands contiguous with the Mediterranean Sea eggplant is a staple vegetable, but the English-speaking peoples have never taken kindly to it. We have not even a name for its handsome fruits, contenting ourselves with the name of an ornamental type of the same plant which bears fruits not unlike large eggs.

It is not as though the species were unfamiliar, for both the purple-fruited and the white have long been cultivated in our gardens, and in England longer still. "These apples have a mischievous quality, the use thereof is utterly to be forsaken," says John Gerard in his famous *Herball*, 1597, voicing the long-held belief that is reflected in its botanical name *melongena*, derived through the Italian *melanzana* from *mala insana*, mad apples. This undeserved appellation was formerly the plant's common name, doubtless from its belonging to the Solanaceae or Deadly Nightshade family. Our Southern nickname of gunny squash or guinea squash seems none too flattering either.

Eggplant must have summer weather and lots of it, for it is a warm-weather, slow-maturing species. It is extensively grown in Florida for shipment and is found in a good many gardens except in the more northerly states.

Varieties

Black Beauty is the standard, bearing four or five large purplish-black fruits of more or less globe shape. Lighter in color and longer in shape is New York Improved. The Southern growers have Florida High Bush, and New Hampshire Hybrid was recently introduced for the North. While early, it has the disadvantage of bearing most of its fruits on the ground.

Culture

A warm, sandy, well-drained soil is best for eggplant, and any manure or compost worked into it should be thoroughly rotted. Only in the far South can seeds be sown in the field, and most growers must begin by sowing in flats two months ahead of transplanting. The sand flat is best, and when the seedlings are nearly two inches high they should be pricked out to individual bands or pots, or set four inches apart each way in a soil flat, so that they may be transplanted to the garden with the least possible disturbance of their roots when they are five or six inches high, after being hardened off. Not only should the soil be warm when eggplants are set out, but the danger of cold nights should be past. The plants should be set two feet apart, with three feet between rows, and the soil given a good sprinkling if it is not sufficiently damp. A handful of 5-10-5 fertilizer may be set in a circle and worked into the ground around each plant when it has become established.

Cultivation should be frequent, as it is important that weeds be prevented from establishing themselves before the plants grow and spread their shallow roots.

The fruits are edible even when half size, and if they are kept picked—or, rather, cut off, for the stems are woody—the plant will continue to develop others.

Diseases

Several forms of wilt are experienced in the commercial production fields, causing yellowing and wilting of the foliage. The only control is crop rotation, as the organisms survive in the soil.

Fruit rot, a fungous disease, is especially troublesome in the South. Discolored spots may appear on any part of the plant or fruit, which may drop prematurely. Repeated spraying with Bordeaux mixture gives good results.

Insects

The eggplant flea beetle may do so much damage to young plants as to stunt them and cause the blossoms to drop. Rotenone or pyrethrum insecticidal dust is effective. Colorado potato beetles and eggplant tortoise beetles also may cause some damage, but dust may be used.

ENDIVE

Cichorium endivia

Endive is grown as a salad herb in its own right and by some as a substitute for lettuce in summer weather, but most frequently it is used in late fall and early winter. It is a hardy plant, unharmed by a little frost.

Varieties

There are two types: one with deeply cut and curly leaves, used for salads—Green Curled being the best known—and one with broad, solid leaves which is used either as a pot or salad herb, Full Heart being the best of these, and commonly known as escarolle.

Culture

For all practical purposes the culture of endive is the same as that of lettuce, the seed being sown in several lots to provide a continuous supply as desired. But an extra process is necessary with endive for salad as it should be blanched to improve both texture and flavor. On a dry day, when there is no rain or dew within the heads, gather the outside leaves around the heart, put a piece of waterproof paper over the top, and tie the whole. In two to three weeks of warm weather, longer when cooler, the heads will be blanched. Tie the heads a few at a time.

In late fall endive may be taken up with a ball of earth around the roots and transplanted to a cool cellar, where growth can be continued and blanching effected by an upturned box if the cellar is not dark.

FENNEL

Foeniculum dulce

Despite the *dulce* in its botanical name this is not Sweet Fennel, which is *F. vulgare,* but a vegetable somewhat reminiscent in texture of celery, with a pronounced anise flavor and an unusual shape as the enlarged leaf bases, which are the edible part, overlap one another, forming a more or less oval "apple." From these bases arise stems carrying graceful, feathery foliage in the manner of asparagus at its summer stage and diffusing a distinct odor of anise.

Seeds are sown in the row, a little at a time, as the plant matures quickly. It requires no attention after thinning out to six inches apart until the leaf bases become sizable, when they are to be blanched by earthing up. They are eaten either raw or cooked, as an aromatic celery might be.

GIRASOLE

Helianthus tuberosus

When Samuel Champlain touched at Cape Cod in 1604 he was given by the Indians, among other vegetables, some roots which he recorded as having the taste of artichokes. It is unfortunate that instead of this trivial comment he did not record the Indian name of the novelty, for it was sun-root, an admirably descriptive term.

Later the roots were introduced to Europe, and the best explanation of their usual absurd name is that they were grown at Ter Neuzen in Holland for the London market, where the hawkers crying their wares soon doubled the misnomer into Jerusalem artichoke.

The French name "Girasole" more accurately describes this native American sunflower, which will grow anywhere and yields tuberous roots smaller than the average run of potatoes and of somewhat turniplike texture when boiled. Baked or boiled and served with a good sauce it is a palatable vegetable, makes an agreeable pickle in sweetened vinegar with small onions, and is a useful foundation for soups. Its carbohydrates are not in the form of starch but occur as inulin, which is easily converted into levulose sugar. The tubers are planted in the spring, eighteen inches apart, either whole or cut, as are seed potatoes, and this is all that need be said about culture, for the plants need no more than do other sunflowers.

But they must be dug up in the fall, for if left to themselves they will overrun the garden. A touch of frost will not harm the tubers and they may be left in the storage shed until required, covered with enough soil to prevent them from drying out.

HORSE–RADISH

Armoracia rusticana

Those who like horse-radish sauce need have no trouble in raising supplies for the manufacture of this pungent condiment. The plant, a perennial with parsnip-like roots, is always grown from cuttings of side roots. These are trimmed with one end square, the other sloping to show it is to point downward in the soil. They should be set in early spring, about twelve inches apart, on a slant rather than upright, and about three inches deep. Commercial growers who seek large roots sometimes draw soil away from the roots early in the season and trim off the side roots, but the home gardener should have quite satisfactory roots if the soil is well manured and fertilized.

A few roots at a time are dug after they have attained full size in fall.

Maliner Kren is the best variety.

KALE

Brassica oleracea var. *acephala*

One of the amenities of the vegetable garden is the decorative effect that can be introduced by a border of curly green kale, a plant that should be more extensively cultivated both for beauty and because it stands in the highest rank in regard to vitamin and dietetic value. When the rest of the garden begins to suffer dilapidation in fall, the kale still stands and provides the best of greens after frost has laid other potherbs low. A still more colorful variety is the variegated or flowering kale, tinted with attractive pastel colors from emerald green to purple, but not of such good table quality as the curlies famed in Scotland's songs and stories.

Varieties

Dwarf Green Curled is probably the most extensively grown, then Dwarf Blue Curled. In the South a blue-green, less curly form is popular: Dwarf Siberian, also known as Sprouts.

Culture

Kale, especially for the winter crop, is usually sown in the garden row, with which exception its culture is the same as that of cabbage. When mature, the whole plant is not cut; leaves are taken as required, beginning from the bottom, and they should not be allowed to grow so old as to be fibrous and tough.

It is subject to the same diseases as cabbage but seems to have more resistance; the cabbage worm and sundry aphids which attack it can be controlled with rotenone or pyrethrum dusts.

KOHLRABI

Brassica oleracea var. *caulorapa*

As its name indicates, this is one of the cole plants and it is an odd-looking one, for just above the surface of the soil its stem swells to the size and shape of a small, round turnip, from various parts of which arise large leaves on long, thin stems. The swollen stem, which is cooked and served as turnip would be, is the part for which the plant is cultivated.

Kohlrabi is a hardy vegetable, unharmed by light frost and better able to withstand drought than turnip, which it may occasionally replace for that reason. Its quality is much better, however, when it makes rapid growth, and for this reason the soil should be rich.

White Vienna is the variety generally grown, but

some gardeners prefer Purple Vienna as it is thought to swell a little larger before beginning to get woody and tough. The light purple tint is only on the surface; the flesh is greenish white. A packet of either will be sufficient for a row of fifty feet or more.

Seed is sown sparsely in the garden row, a little at a time, for continuous supplies, lightly covered, firmed down, and sprinkled. The seedlings are later thinned out once or twice, so that the plants eventually stand six inches apart. When the stem has grown to about two and a half inches in diameter the whole plant is pulled up and the leaves and roots cast on the compost heap.

As a near relative of cabbage, kohlrabi may be attacked by similar enemies, to be similarly controlled.

LEEK

Allium porrum

Leek is a mildly flavored member of the onion family, little grown in American gardens, but esteemed by those who know its blanched stems as a valuable constituent of soups and stews or served in the same style as asparagus. In the garden, it has the merit of being very hardy and, where frosts are not severe, may be left in the garden all winter, providing continuous supplies for the kitchen.

Of the few varieties usually available, Large Flag is the most common, but Giant Musselburgh, developed at the town of that name in Scotland, where leeks are best grown, is hardier and larger.

Seedlings may be started indoors if earlier and larger leeks are wanted, but usually the seed is sown in a shallow trench in the garden, about six inches deep, lightly covered, and firmed down. Being of very thrifty nature, leek will find some sort of living in almost any soil, but the only stems worth growing are thick and succulent, such as require a well-prepared seedbed with supplies of food and moisture easily reached by the small roots.

The plants should stand nine inches apart in the row if large stems are sought, otherwise six inches will suffice, and when they are seven or eight inches high the trench should be gradually filled in around the stems to effect blanching up to where the leaves diverge. Or paper collars may be used, first placed around the seedling, then moved up as the plants grow and earth banked in below them. Leeks sown in early spring will be ready by midsummer. Where winters are too severe to leave any plants in the garden, leeks may be transplanted with a ball of earth around the roots to boxes in the cellar.

LETTUCE

Lactuca sativa

With the coming of spring, fancy turns to thoughts of salad, a deep-seated desire born of ancient after-winter need and immemorial habit. Lettuce is therefore one of the first crops on the home gardener's calendar. Too often it is also one of the first to disappoint him, but it is not difficult to raise successfully if these fundamental facts are borne in mind and operations conducted accordingly:

Salad crops to be crisp must be grown quickly, so the soil should be rich in plant food.

Lettuce has a poor root system, therefore this plant food must be readily available in the upper surface of the soil.

It is essentially a cool-weather plant, unharmed by light frost but rarely withstanding summer heat, and is to be sown, or set out, as soon as the ground can be worked.

There are three main types:

Leaf lettuce: The plant forms a loose head of large, frilly, wavy leaves, of which a few at a time are cut and are later replaced by new growth. Thus this type is labor-saving for the gardener, since no more need be cut than the salad of the day demands. To many it is also the most desirable type, not merely for its flavor and texture, but because a good salad is built upon loose leaves. In addition to all this it is demonstrably higher in vitamin content than is the head type.

Head lettuce: This is the type most commonly found on the markets as its compact, cabbage-like head is well adapted to shipping. Its quality, particularly in modern varieties, is sufficiently satisfactory—at least to those who are content with a quartered head and a spoonful of bottled dressing by way of a salad. For the home gardener, however, it is more difficult to bring to perfection, being more exacting in its needs, less thrifty in adverse conditions, and taking longer to reach the cutting stage. The whole head, of course, is then removed and the plant is gone forever.

Cos lettuce: There are some few who find Cos, or Romaine, the most attractive type because of its longer, smoother, darker leaves. It is a rather more robust plant, standing tall and straight by comparison with the others, and commonly reputed to be more resistant to heat, though this is not always confirmed by experience.

Preparation

The soil should be limed if it is necessary to correct acidity, and it must be thoroughly worked to pulverize all lumps or clods. It should be rich, preferably from heavy manuring in the previous season, but rotted manure or compost may be added if available, together with a good commercial fertilizer at the rate of one pound to twenty feet of row. The organic matter so supplied will hold moisture, which is essential to lettuce, though it cannot tolerate being waterlogged, and the seedbed must therefore be well drained. Nitrate of soda is frequently used to promote rapid and luxurious growth.

Varieties

Scores of varieties may be found in the catalogs, some old, some new, some differing little from others in anything but name. The following are well established, in demand among experienced gardeners, and therefore readily available:

Leaf type: Probably the most popular is Grand Rapids —quick growing and crisp, with light green leaves. Prize Head is of fine quality, but the leaves, which are tinged with reddish brown, are thin and apt to be damaged by heavy rains. Early Curled Simpson and Black-Seeded Simpson are also favorites in American gardens everywhere.

Head type: Among the older varieties, May King is early, with head on the small side; Hanson is larger but considerably later in maturing. These are widely grown in the East. The old New York is a standard in most areas. But the economic importance of huge commercial crops has led to the development in recent years of valuable new varieties, in general intended to thrive better in summer heat, though some have been bred to suit the climatic conditions of different areas. Of these Imperial 847 is the most widely adaptable and is a fine strain of the New York or Iceberg type. Imperial 44 does well in many parts of the North, and in the South for spring and fall sowing.

Another sort of head lettuce is the butterhead, with

thicker, smoother, more succulent leaves, dark green out-side and folding over a compact yellow heart. Big Boston is the most popular, but those who dislike its bronzed tinge usually sow White Boston instead.

Cos type: White Paris, known also as Trianon, is the variety in common use in America, though many others are grown in Europe. Good strains of this are self-folding and do not require the frequently quoted ad-monition that the outer leaves must be tied over the head.

In ordering seed, one packet may be allowed for fifty or sixty feet of garden row.

Sowing

Leaf lettuce is usually sown directly in the garden row, but head lettuce is started indoors. Sow the seeds thinly in rows two inches apart and three weeks later, when the seedlings are about two inches high, prick them out to two inches apart each way. Let them have as much sunlight as possible, behind glass, of course, until within a fortnight of transplanting time, when they should be given a little and a little more exposure in the open air for hardening.

Culture

The garden rows may be as close together as twelve inches but are better at eighteen, and the young plants may be eight to ten inches apart for leaf lettuce; ten to twelve inches for head lettuce or Cos. They should neither stand in a furrow, which will collect water, nor should they be earthed up. As they grow, the soil should be regularly cultivated, which will aerate it, break up any surface caking formed after rain, and keep down the inevitable weeds. If the weather becomes so dry that water should be applied, it may advantageously be manure water—as in such circumstances the plants may require some stimulation—or eight ounces of nitrate of soda to fifty feet of row may be worked in near the plants and watered. As summer heat begins to strike, a shade of sacking erected on a light frame will help to keep the heads from turning tough and bitter prior to projecting seed stalks.

At the time of transplanting, seed may also be sown in a row for later plants. Only a short section at a time should be sown, very lightly covered with soil, tamped down, and kept damp. When the plants are thinned out, those that are large enough may be transferred to another row.

Planting for fall lettuce, which is often postponed until too late because of prevailing abundance of other vegetables, is usually direct in the row, which should then be shaded from the violence of the sun. But just as the seedlings of spring were protected from cold by being started indoors, so now they may equally benefit through similar protection from heat.

Harvest

When lettuce is finally ready to be cut, it is well to take it in the morning with the dew still on it and keep it in the icebox or a very cool place until the salad bowl is ready for this best foundation of all good salads— fresh, home-grown lettuce.

Diseases

Lettuce is subject to a number of blights and rots, often serious in the commercial growing areas but unlikely to menace the average garden. They are usually controlled by crop rotation and the planting of disease-resistant strains. Tipburn is caused by high temperatures with high humidity and shows as a browning along the edges.

Insects

Little damage from insects is suffered by lettuce, especially spring lettuce. Aphids are occasionally troublesome, and the cabbage looper, a little green caterpillar which humps its back, may sometimes be seen on it. Both may be controlled by rotenone or pyrethrum dust. If there are slugs in the garden they will eagerly seek out young lettuce plants, but are deterred by dry ashes, a protective ribbon of slaked lime, or soot. Cutworms are to be destroyed by poisoned bran.

MUSKMELON : CANTALOUPE

Cucumis melo

Some confusion exists as to the terms "muskmelon" and "cantaloupe." The latter was originally a green, warted melon brought by missionaries from western Asia to the papal gardens at Cantalupo, near Rome, and melons of this type, *C. melo* var. *cantaloupensis*, are still extensively grown in Europe. In America, however, cantaloupe usually means a muskmelon of the rather solid, compact, heavily netted type which commercial growers have found necessary for satisfactory shipping. Botanically the muskmelon is *C. melo* var. *reticulatus*.

Preparation

Melons are only for the large garden and the determined gardener who will give his vines the cultural attention they require from the outset and will fight voracious insects for them. A long, sunny hot season, with dry atmosphere but sufficient soil moisture, a light but well-manured soil with mildly acid reaction, pH 6.0 to 6.7, are the desiderata for muskmelons.

Varieties

Bender's Surprise is probably the best known of the larger varieties for the garden and Delicious is a smaller-fruited strain of this, maturing about ten days earlier.

Tip Top is also a large melon; Honey Rock, Pride of Wisconsin, and Hearts of Gold are smaller. There are many others, preferences varying in different districts. Of the shipping melons, or cantaloupes, Hale's Best, an almost round, thick-fleshed, medium-sized variety, is by far the most extensively grown.

In the South and Southwest, casabas or winter melons are sometimes grown. These are relatively smooth-skinned, with pale green flesh, and require a long growing period; Honey Dew is the best known.

Sowing

In the South and Southwest seed is sown in the garden, but sometimes there and nearly always elsewhere plants are started under glass a month before transplanting time, the seeds being set in bands or pots, as seedlings are sensitive to disturbance of their roots. They should be transplanted when small and the soil must be warm, so that growth will not be checked.

Hills are made, five or six feet apart each way, by burying one or two forkfuls of well-rotted manure. Three plants are set in each hill, the weakest of the three to be thinned out later. Plant protector caps are advisable until the vines begin to run, for the young plants are tender and should be shielded from wind as well as cold, but a slit in the cap on the leeward side is necessary in order to allow ventilation. Cultivation should be shallow and may be discontinued as the vines cover the ground.

In dry areas, irrigation is often necessary to supply sufficient moisture until the fruits are formed.

Harvest

The melons are ready at what is called full slip, that is when they part readily from the vine if gently pulled. A good yield would be about half a dozen fruits per plant.

Diseases and Insect Pests

The enemies of cucumber are those of melon also, and in addition the melon worm, a mottled green-and-yellow caterpillar about an inch long, burrows into the fruits. Rotenone and pyrethrum dusts give some control. Melon aphids are troublesome in the South, feeding on the underside of the leaves. Nicotine or rotenone sprays and dusts are effective against these sucking insects.

MUSTARD

Brassica juncea

This is not the mustard which grows so large that "the birds of heaven come and lodge in the branches thereof" or provides the fiery flour used in table mustard, but is an easily grown salad and potherb especially popular in the South.

The variety chiefly grown is Southern Giant Curled; another very similar is Ostrich Plume or Fordhook Fancy. Seed is sown in the garden, a little at a time, in spring and fall; the seedlings come up quickly and are thinned to stand about three inches apart. Within a month they should be four inches high and may then be cut for salad or at six inches high for greens. About an inch of stem is left, so that the plants may put up new leaves.

A packet of seed will supply enough for the average garden.

OKRA

Hibiscus esculentus

A familiar plant in Southern gardens, grown to a limited extent in the North; of very easy culture and ornamental enough to be a good screen at the garden side. Its long pods are used, green or dried, in stews and gumbo, formerly gobbo, soup, or as a vegetable dish if picked young, though their rather mucilaginous texture is not agreeable to everyone.

Okra is by nature a tropical plant and should have continuous hot weather but will grow in any decent soil, and all the better if fertilizer has been added. Seeds are sown an inch deep where the plants are to stand and thinned to twelve inches apart for the dwarf type, eighteen inches for the tall.

Dwarf Green, two to three feet high, is the earliest; Tall Green is the usual tall variety and a strain of this, Clemson Spineless, is about the best of the long, green-podded type. White Velvet has pale green pods.

Although the pods grow to six or seven inches in length, they should be picked regularly so that pods do not approach maturity, and the bearing season will thus be prolonged.

ONION

Allium cepa

Herodotus, the Father of History, tells that in his time there was an inscription on the Great Pyramid, which was constructed more than five thousand years ago, stating that sixteen hundred silver talents had been paid for onions, radishes, and garlic eaten by the builders. Old as this record is, there is evidence that the cultivation of onion is older still, and that through the ages it has been one of man's favorite crops. It is found in most American gardens, though it is not too easy to grow and often brings disappointment because its cultural requirements have not had sufficient attention, particularly in the matter of weeding.

Preparation

The part of the garden chosen for onions should preferably be one which was as free as possible from weeds in the previous season, and they frequently follow carrots, beans, corn or, in the South, cowpeas. The soil should be worked into fine tilth, without clods, stones, etc., to a depth of about six inches, and well enriched. New manure must not be used, but if rotted or composted it is very suitable, and commercial fertilizer may be added at the rate of five pounds to a hundred feet of row, or more if old manure is not available. On large commercial crops an analysis of 5-10-10 is often used on medium soils. Onions cannot be successfully grown on acid soils, and a reaction of pH 6.0 to 6.5 is desirable.

Culture

Early onions are grown from sets, which are small, immature bulblets of the previous season's growth. For later onions, and particularly those intended to be kept in winter storage, seedling plants are bought or raised indoors and transplanted; seed may be sown in the open.

Scallions, or bunching onions, are stalks with little or no bulb, eaten fresh. These are procured by using immature bulb onions, or by planting the non-bulbing perennial species *Allium fistulosum*. There are also two unusual types: the top or tree onion, which bears bulblets, like sets and similarly planted, on top of its stalks; and the multiplier or potato onion, in which the bulb has several cores instead of one, each of which develops into a bulb, thus forming a cluster. These are separated and planted in the fall.

Varieties

Sets are not usually distinguished by variety names but merely by color: yellow, white, or red. They should not be smaller than a half inch in diameter or larger than an inch, and a pound is the usual allowance for a hundred feet of row. For onions raised from seed there is a wide choice of varieties, and local conditions of climate and soil will to some extent determine which are best to grow.

The favorite Yellow Globe is to be had in a number of different strains, as Yellow Globe Danvers, Ohio Yellow Globe, Southport Yellow Globe, Brigham Yellow Globe, and others. The large Sweet Spanish or Valencia is grown extensively in Western mountain states. Of the white-skinned varieties Southport White Globe and Silverskin are standard, with the little White Pearl grown for pickling. The red-skinned varieties are favored for storage, Red Wethersfield is strongly flavored, Southport Red Globe much milder. Ebenezer is a yellow-skinned flattened globe onion much used for sets. Prizetaker is one of the largest in general use.

The mild Crystal Wax and Yellow Bermuda are well adapted to Southern gardens, especially where onions are planted in fall. White Welsh and Nebuka are bunching onions which do not form bulbs.

Sowing

Sets are planted as early in the season as the soil can be made ready, just below the surface and three or four inches apart, for bulb onions, half that distance or less for green bunching onions, and in rows twelve to fifteen inches apart. The same rates apply to seedling plants, which are usually set out a couple of weeks later, when the soil has become a little warmer. Though these plants can, of course, be raised in flats or frames, most home gardeners find that the small expense incurred in their purchase is well justified. The practice of planting thickly and thinning out for scallions is not recommended, as it disturbs the roots of the plants that are left; plant each kind separately.

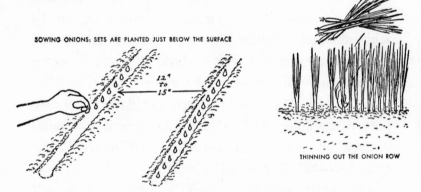

SOWING ONIONS: SETS ARE PLANTED JUST BELOW THE SURFACE

12" to 15"

THINNING OUT THE ONION ROW

For the late crop, seed is sown in the row as early as possible and lightly covered. The soil should be firm, as onions cannot grow when it is loose and powdery. The rate of thinning will depend upon whether the seedlings are intended to produce green onions or bulbs. It is not necessary to make repeated sowings of onions for succession.

Cultivation

It is essential that the rows be kept free of weeds from the outset, as onions grow slowly and have little foliage to create restraining shadow. They have shallow, sparse roots, and cultivation therefore should be little more than a stirring of the surface soil to kill weeds in their early stages and prevent any caking through drying out after rain. This work should be done close to the plants by hand, as the bulbs may easily be injured if struck with the blade of a hoe. Small tools are available for such close work.

Harvest

Green onions or scallions are pulled as and when desired; bulb onions are usually left until full growth has been attained and the tops begin to shrivel, though some gardeners endeavor to hasten this process by breaking down the tops with the back of a rake. To cure the bulbs, they are left in the sunlight or spread on a dry floor until the stems are quite shriveled; these are then cut off within an inch of the bulbs, which may be stored in a cool, ventilated room. Immature onions do not keep, but ripe, well-cured bulbs are solid and naturally adapted to retaining their good qualities, since onions are biennial plants. Bulbs with very thick necks are often discarded because they cure slowly and are more liable to be attacked by the organisms of rot.

Diseases and Insect Pests

Onion smut, mildew, and pink root are fungous diseases with which commercial fields are sometimes infected, but are seldom of importance in the home garden.

One insect is a serious pest: the onion thrips, a very tiny yellowish fly which lays its eggs in the lower part of the leaves, where the young nymphs suck the plant juices, so that when the infestation is severe, usually in dry weather, the leaves look bleached. Spraying with 4 per cent rotenone or nicotine sulphate is effective, but the insecticide should get down into the sheaths of the leaves.

In the North, the onion maggot is destructive. It is the larva of a small gray fly, something like the housefly, which lays its eggs on or near the base of the plant, after which the grubs attack the stems and work their way into the bulbs. A spray of 2 per cent lubricating oil emulsion, which can be bought ready for use after dilution, is sprayed on the soil around the plants when the flies appear, and twice thereafter at intervals of a week or ten days.

PARSLEY

Petroselinum hortense

Parsley is so easy to grow and so much used for flavoring and garnishing that a short row of it should be in the garden, where it will continue through the winter in the South. In the North a few plants may be continued indoors as window plants.

Seed is sown in the row as early as possible and may

be soaked overnight first, as it is slow germinating. The plants may later be thinned to about six inches apart.

The principal variety is Moss Curled, very decorative and the best for garnishing, but Plain is sometimes grown, to be used only for flavoring. About fifteen or twenty plants will be ample, and leaves are picked as required through the season.

Rooted parsley, or heimischer, is occasionally grown for flavoring. It has a root like a small parsnip and may be similarly grown.

PARSNIP

Pastinaca sativa

Parsnip is a cool-weather, long-season plant, better adapted to the climatic conditions of the North than of the South. Though one of the easiest vegetables to grow and one of the most nutritious, it has not attained great popularity, possibly because its large, sweetish roots are not always prepared in the kitchen as they should be, possibly because the plants occupy a garden row all season long and into the winter.

If forked roots are to be avoided, the soil must be well and deeply worked, clods broken up, and rocks removed; it should also be enriched, but by no means with new manure. Only fresh seed should be used, as its vitality is retained for only a year or two. It is sown early in the garden and covered a quarter to half an inch deep, sometimes accompanied by a few radish seeds, for they will come up long before the slow parsnip and mark the row. The radishes will be gone before they can interfere much with the parsnip plants, which will soon thereafter be thinned to about four inches apart.

Apart from necessary cultivation in the earlier stages, they will give the gardener no further trouble until early winter, when they are to be dug, not pulled, as required, and may be left in the row covered with leaves and straw or stored in slightly moist sand in a cold cellar. The roots are seldom injured by frost, nor are they improved, as many suppose. Those that winter in the ground should be dug early in spring lest they run to seed and perpetuate themselves as weeds. The variety generally used is Hollow Crown, but All American, a recent introduction, has roots larger at the shoulder and of medium length. A packet of good seed should be sufficient for fifty feet of row.

GARDEN PEAS

Pisum sativum

Green peas are the gardener's pride and joy. They are among the first rewards of the season, and the garden produces nothing that is at once so nutritious and so delicious. In content they are high in carbohydrates and proteins, with important mineral salts and vitamins in plenty and, to make the ensemble perfect for the most dainty palate, nearly one quarter of the weight of good green peas is sugar. That is, when they are newly picked, as the sugar then quickly begins to change into starch, for which reason, among others, there can never be any peas quite so good as those grown in the home garden. The peas that come to market from far-distant commercial fields have usually been traveling for days and though full of nutriment they have lost with each passing hour more and more of that first fine rapture of sweetness. Accordingly, the good gardener would place peas among the first of his essential crops.

Varieties

The many kinds and varieties of garden peas may be grouped as follows:

Smooth-seeded: In the colder areas, or for extra-early sowing, this type is useful, as it is very hardy and the seed is not so apt to rot in the inhospitable soil under unfavorable conditions as is wrinkled seed. This advantage, however, is gained at the expense of quality, for the peas are small, relatively low in sugar content, and rather thick-skinned. By far the best of these for general garden use is Superb, with low-growing plants bearing pods that are large and plentiful for a variety of this type. It is ready for picking about two months after sowing, in an average spring and under average conditions of growth. Eight Weeks, known also as Radio, is the earliest pea; both pods and peas are smaller than Superb, but it is about ten days earlier. In the most Southern states Creole is valued for its hardiness in both cold and warm weather.

Wrinkled-seeded: It is on this type that the gardener will concentrate, and his choice will be to some extent conditioned by the amount of trouble he is prepared to take in providing supports for the plants. Of the many varieties offered in the catalogs some are much better than others, and while it would be impossible to say that this one or that one is the best in every respect, those in the following selection may be confidently ranked as very good.

The earliest of these is World's Record, standing about two feet high, with plump pods about three inches long. Maturing a week later is Thomas Laxton, to which many experienced gardeners justifiably give the bulk of their early-pea area. It bears the name of a great English pea breeder of the last century, who introduced it about fifty years ago, though its pods were then much lighter colored than they are today as the result of seed-plant selection to that end. The plants are medium tall, about three feet, and bear a profusion of three-and-a-half-inch pods, blunt ended and filled with large, tender peas. A kindred new variety is Teton, slightly larger, a few days later, and wilt-resistant. It received the All-America Silver Medal for 1937.

Good early peas of dwarf growth, and therefore not in need of support, are Little Marvel and Progress. Such small plants, however, cannot bear as many pods as the taller types.

The late peas come into bearing about three weeks after the earliest and yield more abundantly, with bigger peas in larger, pointed pods. Alderman is an excellent tall variety, but it requires trellis or brushwood up to five feet, and therefore Giant Stride (strains of which are known as Asgrow 40, Icer, Wyoming Wonder, etc.) is more popular, as it grows to only half that height. The latest variety, maturing nearly three months after plant-ing, is Improved Stratagem, also of medium height.

These late peas should be grown only in localities where there is a sufficiently long season of reasonably cool weather.

Peas for dry use through the winter are not greatly in fashion now, though commercial acreages are planted in the South, and this provident purpose is best served by White Marrowfat, a very tall, late, smooth-seeded, and hardy variety.

A row of edible-podded peas is worth planting if there is room for it. There is nothing new about this type, but to many people they will be a novelty, and a pleasing one, for the large pods are sweet and succulent. Melting Sugar, with tall plants up to five feet, is the variety usually grown, but a low variety, Dwarf Early Sugar, is also available.

In the South, green peas are often known as English peas, and the term "table peas" is used to dignify a field legume which otherwise goes by the lowlier name of cowpeas, though in reality it would more properly be classed with the beans. While they lack the sweetness and flavor of peas, they make a nutritious and palatable dish, and the crop is further valued because it can be grown in summer on poor land, which it enriches. Sugar Crowder is perhaps the best garden sort; the plants develop quickly, reaching the picking stage in six or seven weeks, and are of low growth, two to three feet, with pods six to seven inches long containing creamy brown peas. Black Eye is a larger variety, grown extensively as a field crop for dried peas but also in gardens for both green and dried use.

Culture

It is not unduly difficult to attain this prize among vegetables that brings a sparkle to the eye of even the most seasoned gardener when it makes its first appearance at table. True, one hears the fainthearted say they never have any luck with peas, but a live seed placed in proper surroundings will germinate and, if the conditions of growth are suitable, will develop into a normal plant fulfilling its natural cycle.

The prime consideration is early preparation of the soil, and this must be thorough, as peas like a good seedbed of mellow earth well worked into fine tilth. This essential task will be one of the first to get winter's stiffness out of the gardener's joints, for it is to be undertaken just as soon as Jack Frost allows. If lime is necessary it can be worked well in at a first rough digging, using the amount indicated by test to reduce acidity to a low point, and it is better to have soil for peas, as for all leguminous plants, a little on the acid side. A week or more should elapse before working in any well-rotted manure or compost that may be available, and this should be thoroughly incorporated, together with whatever fertilizer is to be added. An analysis of 5-10-10, or approximately similar ratio, is usually suitable for peas, as, being legumes, they derive most of their nitrogen supplies from the activities of bacteria which infest their roots. About two pounds per hundred feet of row will usually be sufficient.

Whether the lime or the fertilizer is applied first is not important; the point is that they should not be applied at the same time, because the tendency of the lime is to reduce the availability of phosphorus through the formation of insoluble compounds.

Sowing should not begin for at least a week after completing these preparations, to avoid the possibility of damage to young seedling tissues. In large gardens, however, the practice of commercial growers in regard to fertilizer may well be followed; namely, to apply it as a strip along either side of the row, about three inches away from the seed and one inch deeper. This effects economy while providing ample supplies for the roots.

Seed

In deciding how much to sow, the old rule is to allow about a hundred feet of row for a family of four or five persons. It is not overmuch for one of the very best products of the garden but means as much space, and probably as much time and trouble, as can be spared around the average home. One pound of seed will be ample for this extent of single row, and if more varieties than one are to be used, the amount may be proportioned accordingly.

Inoculation

The nitrogen-fixing bacteria, *Bacillus radicicola*, which live with the pea in symbiosis, or mutually helpful existence, are possibly waiting in the garden soil; they certainly are if peas have been grown there within the past several years. But if the vegetable garden is new, it may be advisable to inoculate the seed by shaking it with a culture of the organisms, purchasable inexpensively at any seed store. The proper strain of bacteria for peas must be used, as those for other leguminous plants not very closely rèlated will be unattracted by the pea roots.

Sowing

Before sowing, the soil is to be well firmed down and consolidated, especially if it is at all light in texture, though not so tightly as to obstruct drainage, of course.

The rows are then marked off with the aid of pegs and line, and one good plan is to make them double rows, six to eight inches apart, with two to two and a half feet to the next double row. The seeds are set staggered or zigzag, thus:

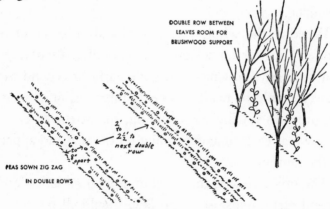

DOUBLE ROW BETWEEN LEAVES ROOM FOR BRUSHWOOD SUPPORT

PEAS SOWN ZIG ZAG IN DOUBLE ROWS

A double row like this leaves room for brushwood to be set in the middle and this should be done either at sowing or very shortly afterward, so that the young plants may have something to climb upon as soon as their first tendrils appear.

An objection to this plan is the difficulty of weeding and cultivating between the halves of the double row after the plants have become more than a few inches high.

The distance between any two seeds is about an inch and a half, though some gardeners prefer to allow more. The depth to plant varies with circumstances, but pea seeds are frequently buried too deeply. In spring, if the soil is moist, they should not be sunk much below an inch; if the surface is dry, about another half inch. Summer sowing for late crops should be deeper, so that there may be sufficient moisture and protection. Finally, the surface should be well trodden down and sprinkled.

Whether the whole pea plot should be sown at one time is a matter on which opinions differ. One view is that successive sowings of a good early or second early variety should be made at weekly intervals, or as soon as the previous sowing has come up, the extent of row to be sown at each time depending on the size and appetite of the family.

The other view is that seed of several varieties, early, second early, midseason, and late, should all be sown at the earliest possible time so as to get the plants well away to an early start and make good growth while the weather is cool.

Possibly the best plan for the medium-sized garden is to compromise with two varieties and make two or three sowings of each.

Cultivation

Weeding around peas in the row is difficult and largely a finger-and-thumb operation which needs to be done with care, especially when the plants are young, or more harm than good will result. It is worth the trouble involved, however, particularly in the early stages of growth, when the weeds can more easily be prevented from obtaining a foothold.

If a dry spell comes, the peas should be supplied with sufficient water, and if growth is unduly slow a ribbon of plant food or fertilizer may be run parallel with the row in a little trench three or four inches away from the plants.

Harvest

To have garden peas at their best they should not be allowed to become fully mature, though the pods must be well grown and plumply filled. They should not be picked until just before they are required in the kitchen.

Insect Pests

The pea aphis is the only insect likely to give trouble in most localities, and when it comes it should be promptly attacked with rotenone or similar dust, as these pests multiply very rapidly and can shrivel a plant by sucking the juices from it.

PEPPER

Capsicum frutescens

Peppers can hardly be considered suitable for the small garden or for one based primarily on nutritive values, but fruits of the sweet varieties are much used in salads and for baking when stuffed; those of the pungent varieties in pickles and condiments. The neat, low, bushy plants are therefore common in larger gardens where the summer is long enough and warm enough.

Varieties

There are many types of peppers, but those of interest to the vegetable gardener fall into two classes, sweet and hot. Of the sweet varieties, California Wonder is the leader, with smooth, large, blocky fruits that can be stood on end without falling over while being prepared in the kitchen. It is of rather long season, however, and in more northerly areas the early strains which have been developed should be planted. World Beater is somewhat similar, larger but not so compact. Ruby King is the longer, thinner type. Pimento is a neat, heart-shaped pepper extensively grown in California and the Southeast, but chiefly for commercial canning. Sunnybrook is tomato-shaped, sweet, and mild.

The hot varieties are much less common in gardens. Long Red Cayenne, with slender pods of about five inches, Red Chili, and Tabasco are used for sauces; Red Cherry for pickles.

A packet of seed will produce more plants than the average garden can accommodate.

Culture

For all practical purposes peppers are grown similarly to eggplants. Seedlings may be raised indoors, but when the popular varieties are to be grown many gardeners prefer to buy young plants of these, which are commonly on sale in the spring. Diseases and insects are unlikely to cause trouble, though flea beetles may need to be kept away from young plants.

POTATO

Solanum tuberosum

To most gardeners, potato and Irish potato are synonymous terms, but in the warmer regions of the South, potato needs the adjective as, being less well adapted to growing conditions there than the sweet potato, the latter is more often known as potato.

The potato is not Irish, it is native American, but its importance in our agriculture dates from its return with settlers from Ulster in the eighteenth century and was accelerated by the influx of immigrants following the famine caused in Ireland by potato blight in 1846.

Even in the more temperate areas of the country, potatoes are much less frequently planted in gardens than formerly. They require a lot of space and fertilizer but do not yield proportionately; they are subject to many diseases and attacked by many insects; on the other hand, they are in constant supply at the stores, since improved technical knowledge and equipment have led to vastly increased commercial production and efficient distribution.

Preparation

The soil for potatoes must be well prepared, preferably begun by deep digging or plowing in the previous fall, and finished to a fine tilth in early spring. An acid soil, with reaction of pH 5.0 to 5.5, is best both for yield and for freedom from scab.

Shallow trenches about six inches deep are open two feet apart for early potatoes, three feet for main crop, and fertilizer of high potash analysis such as 5-8-10 is worked in at the rate of fifteen pounds to a hundred feet of trench. Unfertilized soil must then be thrown in so that the seed potatoes may not come in contact with the fertilizer lest it burn them.

Varieties

The many varieties of potato exhibit a diversity of shape, size, and color but are broadly divided into early and late. Irish Cobbler, a more or less round shape with creamy white skin, is a good old early; Chippewa, also roundish and cream-colored, is resistant to mild mosaic. Of the late or main crop varieties, Green Mountain is one of the best known, with large, flattened, oblong, light russet tubers; Katahdin, recently developed for mosaic-resistance, is smooth, rounded, and with creamy skin.

Seed potatoes should be bought only from a reliable source and be certified disease-free stock. Many growers also treat the tubers with corrosive sublimate solution, two tablets per quart of water, for an hour or two. Eight pounds should be sufficient for a hundred feet of row, yielding two to three bushels.

Planting

The seed potatoes are cut into four or five pieces of good size, each of which must have at least one strong eye, and the rate of planting is one piece per foot and covered to a depth of three to four inches by pulling soil in to fill up the shallow trenches. Shoots will appear in about three weeks.

Cultivation

Cultivation should be light, merely scuffling the weeds off rather than digging them out, in order to avoid cutting shallow roots, and soil is gradually drawn up to the plants as they grow.

Harvest

When the tubers are mature the tops wither, and digging may follow any time within the next month or so. The potatoes are left in the opened row only long enough to let the soil on them become dry. They are then moved to storage in a cellar which must be dark to prevent them from turning green, and cool, to keep them from sprouting. The best temperature is around 37° F.

Diseases

Though potatoes are subject to many diseases, leaf blight is the most serious and it is to be combated by spraying with 4-4-50 Bordeaux mixture every ten days or so after the plants are four or five inches high. Most of the other diseases can be prevented only by seed disinfection and crop rotation.

Insect Pests

The Colorado potato beetle with yellow-and-black-striped wing cases and its red larvae, which come from clusters of eggs on the underside of leaves, will strip the foliage if unchecked. Dusting with .75 per cent rotenone will kill the larvae and some adults; spraying with 4 per cent rotenone or calcium arsenate, four ounces to six gallons of water, should give control. The latter may be added to Bordeaux mixture used against blight.

Blister beetles, flea beetles, and leaf hoppers will also be restrained by the Bordeaux spray. Potato aphids are controlled by rotenone or nicotine sulphate spray. Wireworms, white grubs and, in the South, potato tuber worms and nematodes are the pests of the tubers.

PUMPKIN

Cucurbita spp.

Pumpkins sprawl over so much territory, requiring even more space than muskmelons, that they cannot be considered as very suitable subjects for garden culture. Small Sugar, about seven inches in diameter and the best variety for pies, may be grown where there is room and to spare. Its requirements are similar to those of musk-melon except that the hills should be a foot farther apart each way.

RADISH

Raphanus sativus

Radish is the simplest of vegetables to grow and the quickest to make returns. It will grow almost anywhere, provided it has enough moisture, but if it is to be crisp, it should have readily available plant food in a rather loose, fine soil.

Varieties

There are three types of radish in garden use. Spring varieties are usually globular in shape as Scarlet Globe, about an inch in diameter; Sparkler, the same but with a white tip; and Crimson Giant, a size larger. Summer radishes do not grow quite so quickly. Long Scarlet is about five inches long; White Icicle, about the same length, but milder in flavor. Winter radishes require about two months for growth. White Chinese and Rose Chinese are about six inches long; Long Black Spanish is cylindrical, seven or eight inches long, of pungent flavor, and keeps well in storage.

Culture

Sow spring radishes as early in the season as desired—a week's supply at a time—thin the plants to stand an inch apart, and keep the weeds under control. Summer radishes require a little more space and the winter sorts should be spaced about three inches.

Harvest

Spring radishes should be pulled directly they attain full size, for if left longer in the soil they become pithy and tough. Summer radishes hold their quality much longer, and winter radishes may be stored for months in a box of moist sand if the temperature is around 40° F.

RHUBARB

Rheum rhaponticum

Rhubarb is one of the perennials of the garden, and where there is room for a few clumps they yield a good return in spring for the small amount of attention they require. More than forty centuries ago the Chinese knew the medicinal virtues of a type of rhubarb grown for its roots, which in time became an important article of commerce, but our garden plant is Russian. It reached England about 1620, where it gradually passed from the apothecary's garden into general cultivation, though it was still a novelty in America a century ago.

The warmer sections of the South are not suitable for rhubarb; elsewhere a planting may endure for twenty years or longer, though after eight or ten years the stalks are likely to become smaller and the roots are then dug up. Those known to be the most productive may be divided and replanted in another spot.

Culture

Though rhubarb can be started from seed, this method is tedious and impractical, as only a few plants are wanted, say six for a family of four or five, and roots are readily purchasable in spring. The best variety is Macdonald, developed comparatively recently for large, well-colored stalks at Macdonald College, Quebec, and since then planted in many parts of the continent.

The roots should be set four or five inches deep, four feet apart, and, as the size and succulence of the stems depend largely on the amount of plant food available, the soil should be well enriched. Weeds should be kept down until the plants shade the area, and no stalks are to be pulled in the first season. In the fall, when the plants die down, a mulch of straw and manure may be laid around them, to be dug in early next spring.

Harvest

Stalks will be available in the second year, and they are not to be broken off, but pulled by grasping the stalk at the base and pulling it out. Not too many stalks should be taken this year, but in succeeding seasons they may be pulled for about eight weeks, or until their quality falls off, indicating that food reserves in the roots are running low. The plants are then left to store up food for another year throughout the summer. Flower stalks will appear and are to be pulled out, as the production of seed deprives the plant of strength.

For winter forcing, roots are dug up in late fall, placed in boxes of soil, and left outside until after a good frost, when they are moved into a dark cellar. Two such plants would probably furnish enough winter rhubarb for the average family.

Diseases and Insect Pests

Rhubarb suffers little from diseases or insects other than the rhubarb curculio, a snout beetle about half an inch long, black, and covered with a yellow dust. It feeds on the leaves and the stalks, making punctures from which sap exudes as drops of gum. The only control is picking by hand, but dock should be eliminated from the neighborhood, as the insect passes part of its life on this weed.

ROCKET

Eruca sativa

Known also as roquette, erucola, and rucola, this salad herb of ancient lineage is now seldom planted, as its horse-radish flavor is of limited appeal. This is not so strong, however, when the plant grows quickly in good soil and a cool season.

Seed is sown in early spring and the leaves, which somewhat resemble those of turnip, will be ready in about six weeks, when the plants are eight inches high. It is also grown in fall, but cannot thrive in hot weather.

SALSIFY

Tragopogon porrifolius

The vegetable oyster, as it is called, not for its habit but for its flavor when cooked—though the resemblance is more fancied than real—deserves to be more generally grown. It is a root of pleasing texture and flavor and is cultivated precisely as parsnip except that salsify, being slimmer, may stand a little closer in the row. It is equally free of diseases and insect pests, requires an equally long or longer growing season, and may be left in the ground all winter without harm. If dug up for storage, an inch or two of tops should be left on the roots.

Scorzonera or Black Salsify, *Scorzonera hispanica*, is similar to salsify but somewhat larger, and the long, white-fleshed root has a blackish exterior.

SEA KALE

Crambe maritima

This excellent vegetable is esteemed one of the choicest products of the garden in England, where its blanched shoots, though of quite different character, rival asparagus in popularity as an early spring dish.

It is a cool-season perennial which may be grown from seed, but much more easily by root cuttings which are set in rich, well-prepared soil three feet apart each way. As with rhubarb, no harvest is possible the first year, and very little the second, but thereafter and for years to come many sprouts will be produced.

In fall the leaves are cleared away and a box or corked pot is set over the crown of each plant, then a layer of manure over this and around, or if manure is not available leaves and earth may be used. In early spring the shoots will grow below the box, which must exclude light, and they are cut close to the root when about six inches high. Cutting continues for about a month, as shoots develop; then the cover is removed and the plants proceed with their summer growth to lay up reserves of food for next season in the roots. Any small blanched stems that remain should be removed, so as to prevent the production of flower stems, which weaken the plant. The winter mulch should be dug in between the plants.

SORREL

Rumex acetosa

This is a dock, occasionally grown for early greens. It is a hardy perennial of easiest culture, grown from seed and ready for first cutting the following spring. The plants are mulched in late fall to protect them from undue cold, and in spring the large, light green, slightly acid leaves appear among the first products of the garden. They are cut within an inch of the soil and will grow again for a second cutting. Through the summer they are allowed to grow, so as to store up reserve food in the roots, and a light application of nitrate of soda may be given. All seed stalks should be removed. The plants will continue for several years.

SPINACH

Spinacia oleracea

Although spinach is not now in such high repute among the dietitians as it was a few years ago, it remains one of the most important potherbs, cultivated everywhere in cool weather—a winter crop in the far South and Southwest, a staple of the spring and fall elsewhere.

Preparation

Any good, well-drained garden soil will suit spinach provided it is not acid, the desirable reaction being pH 6.0 to 7.0. More acid soils should be limed at whatever rate is indicated by the soil test. It is very necessary that digging and pulverizing be thoroughly done and old manure or compost worked in, or commercial fertilizer added.

Varieties

There are two types: one with crumpled leaves, of which Bloomsdale Savoy Long Standing is the most popular; the other has thicker, smoother leaves, as typified by Nobel. Both these are relatively long standing, that is, they are less prone than others to shoot seed-stalks and become inedible. Allow one packet for each thirty feet of row.

Sowing

Spinach is sown in the open as early as possible in the season, setting the seeds an inch apart and a half inch to an inch deep in rows twelve to fifteen inches apart. Weekly or fortnightly sowings should be made, the last one fifty to sixty days before the hot weather of summer is expected, which spinach cannot withstand.

Summer sowing for fall spinach is usually in a row vacated by one of the early crops and, in localities where the winter is not too severe, sowing may be continued into fall, as spinach is hardy and may be carried through the frosts—if mulched with straw, leaves, etc.—to make an early start in the following spring. For fall sowing the disease-resistant Virginia Savoy and Old Dominion are recommended.

Cultivation

The plants are thinned to stand five inches apart in the row, and weeds must be kept down. Some gardeners, to encourage leaf development, add nitrogen halfway through the growing period, troweling in a little nitrate of soda along the row or sprinkling it on the soil in a solution of two ounces to a gallon of water.

Diseases

To guard against damping-off, spinach seed is often treated with red copper oxide or zinc oxide.

Spinach blight shows as a yellowing and mottling of the leaves. This stops growth. It is a virus disease transmitted from one plant to another by insects, and where it is known to be in the neighborhood, the resistant varieties should be planted.

Rusts and molds which sometimes plague commercial growers are not likely to be of importance in the garden.

Insect Pests

Aphids, largely on the underside of leaves, may injure spinach and can be controlled by rotenone or pyrethrum insecticide dust, provided it is efficiently applied.

NEW ZEALAND SPINACH

Tetragonia expansa

This is not spinach, and does not in the least resemble it in the garden, but when cooked and served at table there is little difference between them. It has the great merits of flourishing in summer heat, and as its leaves are picked, others grow to replace them. Its demerits are that it is a sprawling and untidy prostrate plant which sheds seeds profusely in fall, so that it often makes quite unexpected and unwelcome appearances in the following summer.

But it is valuable where summer spinach is relished and it grows very freely. The large seeds are hard and should be soaked for a day before planting them about a foot apart. Growth is slow at first, but the plants spread out to three or four feet and endure, unharmed by diseases or insects, until frost comes.

SQUASH

Cucurbita spp.

The extensive family of squashes falls into two broad classes: the bush or summer type, growing compactly, by comparison, and producing fruits which are eaten while immature, and the vine or winter type, which sprawl widely and produce fruits eaten at maturity.

The current divisions of pumpkins and squashes are traditional rather than scientific. True squashes have soft, smooth fruit stems at maturity; pumpkins have hard, woody, ridged stems, usually enlarged at the point of attachment. According to this botanical classification, what are commonly known as summer squashes are really summer pumpkins, and the vining squash Table Queen is a pumpkin.

Some of the summer squashes, using the current terminology, are fairly suitable for the medium-sized garden, as they may stand two feet apart if in rows or three to four feet apart if in hills, but the vining or large squashes of autumn and winter require twice as much space, or more, and could be accommodated only in an extensive garden.

Preparation

The soil should be well prepared where the plants are to stand, as they have spreading, shallow roots, and old manure or compost should be worked in, both for plant food and to retain soil moisture. A handful of commercial fertilizer may well be added, or more of it if the compost is not available.

Varieties

Fruits of the summer squashes exhibit considerable diversity of form. Of the cylindrical yellow type, Early Prolific Straightneck is the best though not the largest; of similar type but with bent neck is Summer Crookneck; White Marrow is a creamy, cylindrical English type; Zucchini and Cocozelle are Italian marrows with variegated green exteriors; Bush Scallop, white or yellow, is small, circular, and scalloped around the edge.

Of the vining squashes, one has become very popular because of its small neat fruits which when baked are sufficient for two people, this is Table Queen. Among the large winter squashes for storage Golden Delicious is one of the best, and the various Hubbards are extensively grown by market gardeners.

A packet of any variety will contain enough seed for the average garden.

Culture

When the soil is well warmed, seeds of the bush varieties may be set five or six inches apart, about an inch deep, in rows; for vining squashes five or six seeds are planted to each hill, about an inch deep, to be thinned out later to not more than three plants per hill. Cultivation should be only deep enough to destroy weeds, until the plants shade the area for themselves.

Harvest

The bush-type fruits are picked while still very young, and if the rind is resistant to a thumbnail, they will be too mature and inedible. The large winter squashes are admirable for storage, but not cold storage, where humidity is high; the best temperature range to avoid shrinkage is 40° to 50° F. They should be gathered before frost, cutting the vine, not the fruit stem, and without causing any bruises on the rinds.

Diseases and Insect Pests

Diseases are not likely to be serious in the garden squashes, but insects are troublesome. The squash bug, a hard, brown insect about five eighths of an inch long which diffuses an acrid odor when crushed, should be destroyed in its early stages if possible. Its reddish-brown eggs are to be found in neat groups on the underside of leaves and may be removed. At the next stage the young insects remain close to one another and may succumb to rotenone, pyrethrum, or nicotine insecticides. But when they reach the adult stage they must either be picked off by hand or trapped under pieces of board.

The squash vine borer is a caterpillar about an inch long which tunnels in the stem. Its presence may be detected by the detritus it casts out and if the stem is slit there with a razor blade the worm is apt to meet its end. The main stem is often covered with soil as it runs, to induce the formation of new roots. The larvae before gaining access to the stem may be killed by rotenone dust.

The squash ladybeetle is, like the Mexican bean beetle, a ladybird unfortunately turned vegetarian. It is a dull yellow, marked with twelve black spots; its larva is about three eighths of an inch long, with black spines. The adults feed on the upper side of leaves, the larvae on the underside. Both may be destroyed with rotenone dust.

SWEET POTATO

Ipomoea batatas

The sweet potato is by nativity a tropical plant and can be grown satisfactorily only where summer temperatures both day and night are high and prolonged. Commercial production is highest in Georgia, but ranges from southern New Jersey to California, with crops also grown where favorable conditions exist in limited localities elsewhere. The trailing vines require so much space and the potatoes are so readily available at the stores that for the smaller garden sweet-potato growing is impractical; for the larger garden it is of doubtful economy.

Sweet potato will grow in almost any soil, but it should preferably be light sandy loam, and not so rich as to lead to overproduction of vines and gross potatoes. Preparation should not be deeper than about six inches, and fertilizer added is usually commercial rather than organic, since available manure or compost can be applied more profitably to other crops.

The variety to be grown will depend largely on the district in which the garden is located, as the relatively mealy and dry types, such as Yellow Jersey, suit the more northerly areas, while the moist-fleshed varieties, such as Nancy Hall, Puerto Rico, and Southern Queen, suit the South.

It will also depend on what is available locally for planting. Seed is not practicable for the home gardener, and in the North slips drawn from sprouting seed potatoes are used; in the South either slips, for early potatoes, or vine cuttings for the main crop. It is important that these be procured only from a reliable source as a safeguard against the transmission of diseases.

The plants should be puddled in and covered, the spacing depending on the variety and the soil, but varying from fifteen to twenty inches apart in the row, with from three feet to six feet between rows. A week or two later a top-dressing of special sweet-potato fertilizer, at the rate of about five pounds to a hundred feet of row, may be worked into the soil near the plants.

Although cutworms and other general pests may occasionally be bothersome, the only serious enemy is the sweet-potato weevil, a slender, antlike snout beetle, the larva of which tunnels through the vines to the roots. The only controls are the cleaning up of crop refuse and the use of plants free from the insect.

TOMATO

Lycopersicum esculentum

The tomato is one of the most popular garden plants, one of the most fruitful, and one of the most easily grown. It requires a considerable amount of space but makes good use of it, and the gardener of even a small plot will try to find room for a few plants whatever else he grows. Apart from the richness of the fruits in vitamins and dietetic value, can any tomato ever equal in flavor one newly picked, with the warmth of the sun diffusing the delicate aroma of its subtle esters and ethers? The garden would be incomplete without tomatoes.

Its present popularity was not easily attained. Though a native American, originated in Peru and well known in pre-Columbian Central America, it was only after its reintroduction from Europe in the eighteenth century that it came to be valued in this country, first as an ornamental and then, about 1800, as an esculent. In the Old World it was unknown until the Spanish explorers began to take back seeds of novel plants, but soon thereafter was highly appreciated in southern Europe. In France and England it made slower progress and, as here, came into general use only in the past century.

Preparation

Tomatoes will grow in any decent garden soil, properly drained but retentive of soil moisture, and in good heart. Liming is rarely necessary, the tolerance of tomato to acidity in the soil being from medium acid, with a reaction of pH 5.6, to neutral, pH 7.0.

Varieties

Their name is legion. Each year new names are announced and the old ones are relinquished but slowly, so that the lists get longer and the claims get stronger, until experience has demonstrated the merits of different varieties in the conditions of growth obtaining in diverse parts of the country.

The most popular type of tomato is red in color and approximately spherical in shape. Stokesdale, Marglobe, and Rutgers (arranging them in order of maturity rather than merit) are among the best of the main crop class; Scarlet Dawn of the early class; and for particular conditions, such as the shorter summers of the most northerly states, varieties of limited use have been developed.

Of the pink varieties, which are really purplish pink, the best known is Livingston's Globe, which commemorates in its name a pioneer in tomato development of the past century, A. W. Livingston of Columbus, Ohio.

The yellow tomatoes are regarded as milder and less acid in flavor than the red, and they add a pleasing variation of color to a salad. Golden Queen is the old standard, but the recently developed Mingold is an improvement. The white tomato has long been cultivated as a novelty but has neither deserved nor attained popularity.

Where there is room for them in the garden, the small-fruited varieties are worth growing. They are shaped like cherries, small pears, or plums, in red or yellow, borne profusely, and are always attractive, especially to children, who need no encouragement to help themselves to vitamins in this agreeable form.

The so-called husk tomato or ground cherry, *Physalis pruinosa,* usually included in this class, is not a tomato at all, though its little yellowish, husk-clad fruits have something of the tomato flavor.

A single packet of seeds of each selected variety will provide more than enough plants for any home garden.

Sowing

Six or seven weeks before the arrival of the warm days of spring is expected sow the seed in sand flats or a mixture of sand and soil, three or four to the inch, in rows two inches apart, and after their first true leaves have appeared prick them out into other flats, at a distance apart of three to four inches each way, or into individual pots or bands.

When the garden soil has been well warmed up and frost has definitely gone, the young plants are set out at intervals of not less than two feet, and preferably three feet, the roots a little deeper than they were in the flat or frame, and watered in with starter solution. At the same time, a stake or pole should be set beside each plant, a foot or more in the ground and about five feet high, to which the vine later on must be tied, since it is not naturally a climber but a sprawler. Soft twine that will not restrict growth should be used for the tie. It is first tied tightly around the pole, then loosely around the plant stem. The tender plants may at first be protected with a shade from strong sunshine, or with an upturned flowerpot at night if the air is likely to be chilly.

As the plants grow, suckers or side branches spring from the axils of leaves where they join the main stem. Until fruit is set these are to be pinched out, some gardeners leaving only one stem, others preferring two or three, and when the plant has reached the top of the pole, its terminal is pinched off to stop further growth in that direction.

Another method of growing the plants is to set three short stakes with a barrel hoop tied between them, or to provide a trellis of some sort. In commercial production, and in large gardens, they are usually allowed to sprawl naturally and unpruned. The heavy vine growth mulches the soil and conserves moisture, so that the fruits are less liable to blossom-end rot induced by dry conditions and

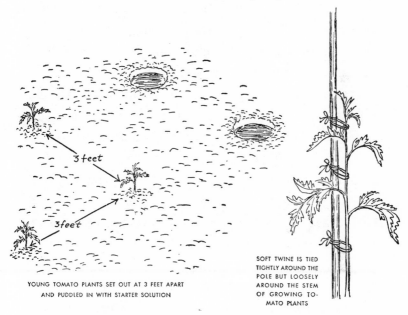

YOUNG TOMATO PLANTS SET OUT AT 3 FEET APART
AND PUDDLED IN WITH STARTER SOLUTION

SOFT TWINE IS TIED
TIGHTLY AROUND THE
POLE BUT LOOSELY
AROUND THE STEM
OF GROWING TO-
MATO PLANTS

they also are less liable to sun scald and cracking. But sprawling plants require more space and are not so easily treated effectively with protective sprays or dust; their fruits are not so large, clean, and conveniently placed.

Cultivation

Cultivation should be shallow but continuous, both to keep weeds down and to conserve moisture in the soil.

Care should be taken that the hoe does not knock the stems of the plants, for they are tender, and disease germs may be admitted.

When the plants have become well established after a week or two in the garden, a handful of complete fertilizer such as 5-8-7 may be worked into the soil in a circle around the stem and about six inches away from it. High-nitrogen fertilizer, such as nitrate of soda, may be helpful when fruit begins to set, but before then may encourage vegetative growth to the detriment of fruiting.

Tomatoes need plenty of water, but when it is supplied the soil should be deeply soaked, not merely wetted on the surface. A tall can with a few nail holes punched in the bottom may be sunk adjacent to a plant and with its top edge a little above the surface of the soil. When this is filled, a slow supply trickles to the roots. Some gardeners spread a mulch of straw around the plants.

Harvest

Fruits should be picked as soon as they are ready throughout the season, so that the plant may be encouraged to continue bearing. With good management the yield per plant should be about eight or ten pounds, and probably a number of green fruits will be on the vine in late fall. The small ones may be saved for pickling, those that are larger and show some red coloration will ripen further if taken indoors.

Diseases

Tomatoes are subject to many diseases but few of them are serious in garden cultivation where the soil is likely to be free from the infecting organisms. Seed treatment will help to control damping-off and certain blights that may be seed-borne. Blossom-end rot, which shows as a yellowish spot and develops into a large, dark brown shrunken area, is chiefly caused by lack of adequate soil moisture in continuous supply. In the South, nematodes may cause the swelling and malformation known as rootknot; these minute pests may be starved out of the soil by growing peanuts, Iron cowpeas, or certain other crops for two or three years. Some other diseases may be kept in check by disposing of plant trash and weeds, spraying with Bordeaux mixture, and restraining the activities of insects.

Insect Pests

In addition to the cutworms, aphids, flea beetles, and other general pests, the tomato hornworm, so called from a projection on its posterior end, is very destructive. It is a huge green caterpillar, three to four inches long, the larva of the sphinx moth, or hawk moth, that hovers at dusk in the manner of a hummingbird as it sips nectar from deep flowers. The worm may be controlled by rotenone dust, and an effective natural check may often be seen in the form of small white cocoons attached to its back. Do not destroy any hornworm so infested, for the cocoons will develop into parasitic larvae, destroying their host and continuing their beneficial race.

The tomato fruitworm is the corn ear worm and the cotton bollworm, its name depending upon where it is found. This also may be checked by rotenone dust.

TURNIP

Brassica rapa

Turnip is an easily grown and productive vegetable, particularly useful in succession cropping, for fall and winter use, but also grown in spring. Turnip tops, prized particularly in the South, are one of the best sources of vitamins in the diet.

Varieties

The most extensively grown is Purple Top White Globe; the flat Purple Top Milan is the earliest; Golden Ball, Cow Horn, and others are also grown for their roots; Seven Top is for greens only; Shogoin makes still better greens, and if the gardener forgets to gather the tops, the roots will be edible a week later. One packet will be enough for the garden.

Culture

Turnip is a cool-weather plant that will grow in almost any garden but makes its best response to a soil that is well worked and in good fertility. Spring sowing in the garden should begin as early as possible, a little of the row at a time in order to provide continuous supply. Sowing should cease, however, two months before summer heat is likely to strike and may begin again two months before the frosts.

Fertilizer applied to the soil for turnip in spring should be high in phosphates, to which it shows marked response; for fall turnips, fertilizer is rarely necessary as enough is likely to be left in the soil after the preceding crop.

The seed should be thinly sown, in rows twelve to fifteen inches apart, lightly covered, and firmed down. The distance the plants should stand apart will depend on the variety but is usually about five inches, and the intermediate young plants may be used for greens.

Aphids are often troublesome, especially on the underside of leaves, but may be controlled by rotenone or nicotine insecticides. The cabbage maggot or root maggot may also attack turnip.

RUTABAGA: SWEDE TURNIP

Brassica napobrassica

Rutabaga is larger, hardier, and firmer fleshed than turnip, and thus more highly valued for winter storage. In appearance they differ considerably, rutabaga being more elongated than any of the globe-shaped turnips, with gray-green, smooth foliage instead of the green, hairy leaves of the turnip.

Varieties

American Purple Top and Golden Neckless are the best-known yellow sorts; Macomber is the best white and worth growing.

Culture

Culture of the two species is similar but rutabaga requires more room in the row, standing seven or eight inches apart, and a month to six weeks longer for maturity.

WATERMELON

Citrullus vulgaris

As watermelon hills of two vines each should be spaced from seven to ten feet apart, depending on the variety and the soil, they are obviously more for the field than the garden.

Varieties

Tom Watson and Kleckley's Sweet are well-known Southern varieties of the long, dark type; Leesburg, dark green, and Hawkesbury, gray, are new wilt-resistant, long melons. Stone Mountain is a large, round-oval, medium-green variety noted for its sweetness, now available also in a wilt-resistant strain. Dixie Queen is of similar shape but longitudinally striped light and darker green.

In California the Klondike group are leaders, green, striped and wilt-resistant green. It is possible to raise watermelons in the more northerly states by using such a variety as the small round Northern Sweet which, as it weighs only about ten pounds, may be described as an icebox melon and grown elsewhere for its convenient size.

Culture

In general, watermelon culture is similar to that of muskmelon, but this plant will tolerate more acid soils, down to a reaction of $pH5.0$, requires a longer season, more space, and even less chance of cool weather.

Diseases

The diseases and insect pests which afflict watermelon are for the most part those of muskmelon also. One of the worst is fusarium wilt, caused by a fungus which spreads from the soil through the water-conducting tissues and clogs them so that the vine dies. To combat this the wilt-resistant varieties mentioned above have been developed.

CHAPTER VIII

Culinary Herbs

The term "herb" applies to any plant that dies to the ground each year and does not become woody or permanent, as in shrubs and trees. Thus we have herbaceous borders, potherbs, and salad herbs, but in current acceptation herbs are garden plants used for flavoring or fragrance. Their culture is often thought a special branch of the gardener's art, as though this might be divided into flowers, herbs, vegetables, shrubs, and trees, yet a number of these herbs may properly be grown in vegetable gardens though they may also be found in plots intended primarily for sweet and aromatic herbs. Some of those summarized as follows are of greater importance in the kitchen than others, but they all add interest and diversity to the vegetable garden.

SWEET BASIL, *Ocimum basilicum:* A bushy, light green annual, fifteen to eighteen inches high. The flower buds and tender leaves are used in soups, tomato dishes, meat seasoning, etc.

BORAGE, *Borago officinalis:* Once introduced, this annual will be found very persistent but makes a pleasant silvery-green border, about fifteen inches high, with bright blue flowers very attractive to bees. The leaves have a flavor of cucumber, formerly thought a cooling addition to summer drinks, and are edible when cooked as greens.

CARAWAY, *Carum carui:* A biennial with finely cut, bluish-green leaves, about a foot high. A hardy plant, but where the winter is cold it should be protected with a mulch. The seeds for which it is grown are produced in the second season.

CHERVIL, *Anthriscus cerefolium:* An annual, about eight inches high, looking and tasting rather like parsley, and similarly grown. A cool-weather plant, to be grown in spring and fall. Turnip-rooted chervil, *Chaerophyllum bulbosum,* has a root about five inches long, black without, yellow within, used for flavoring. It should be sown in fall, mulched over winter, and used in spring.

CHIVE, *Allium schoenoprasum:* A dainty perennial onion grown for its tubular leaves eight or ten inches long. Propagation is usually by bulbs which grow in clumps and are divided and replanted each spring, or some may be grown indoors through the winter.

CORIANDER, *Coriandrum sativum:* A pleasing annual about eighteen inches high, with bright green, finely cut foliage, grown for its seeds which, when dry, have a savor reminiscent of oranges. The umbels or seed heads mature in about two months and should then be removed, as the plant readily reseeds itself.

DILL, *Anethum graveolens:* This herb is of commercial as well as home importance, being put, as John Parkinson wrote in 1629, "with pickled cowcumbers, wherewith it doth very well agree, giving unto the cold fruit a pretty spicie taste or rellish." It should be sown in early spring, and the seedlings later thinned out to about fifteen inches apart. The plant grows to about thirty inches high and its seed heads, seeds, and young leaves chopped are the parts used in compounding dill pickles and sauces.

GARLIC, *Allium sativum:* Properly used, this is one of the most valuable herbs and a good example of the virtue of temperance. Instead of one solid bulb, like onion, it has several cloves—that is, clefts or divisions—in a group covered by a thin skin. Cloves are used for planting in spring or, in the South, in fall, six inches apart, and when the tops wither at maturity the plants are dug, the tops plaited, and hung in an airy place to cure.

MINT, *Mentha spicata:* This is spearmint, one of the many mints but the most extensively used, for mint sauce, mint jelly, and that noble drink of the South. It is a perennial of the easiest culture, started from underground stolons, and spreads quickly. The leaves should be dried in the shade.

SAGE, *Salvia officinalis:* A hardy perennial, bushy plant about eighteen inches high grown for its leaves which, in moderation, are esteemed in stuffings and sausages. Set young plants, which may be raised indoors or bought, two to three feet apart in the perennial corner of the garden. Take few leaves in the first year of growth. Afterward prune the plants two or three times in the course of a season and dry the leaves in the shade, then keep them in airtight containers. Do not cut the plants back before winter. Two or three will suffice when grown.

SAVORY, SUMMER, *Satureia hortensis:* A fragrant annual, about fifteen inches high, grown for its little leaves and flowering tops, which are used in stuffings and boiled with peas or beans. Mix the minute seeds with sand when sowing, so as to get better distribution, and thin the plants later to stand a foot apart.

SAVORY, WINTER, *Satureia montana:* A decorative and pleasant perennial readily grown from seed or cuttings. Thought inferior to summer savory, but it stays green most of the winter even if the leaves are less pungent than in summer.

TARRAGON, *Artemisia dranunculus:* A shrubby perennial about two feet high, and more if not kept cut, grown from cuttings and spaced about two feet apart. The long, narrow leaves are used freshly picked in making tarragon vinegar, in certain sauces, and, to advantage, in salads.

THYME, *Thymus vulgaris:* This is Common or Garden thyme, one of the many thymes, a shrubby perennial standing about ten or twelve inches high, grown for its small aromatic leaves, which are used in seasonings. It is easily grown from division of old plants, less easily from seed, and when in flower the blossoms should be cut with about two inches of stem and dried in the shade.

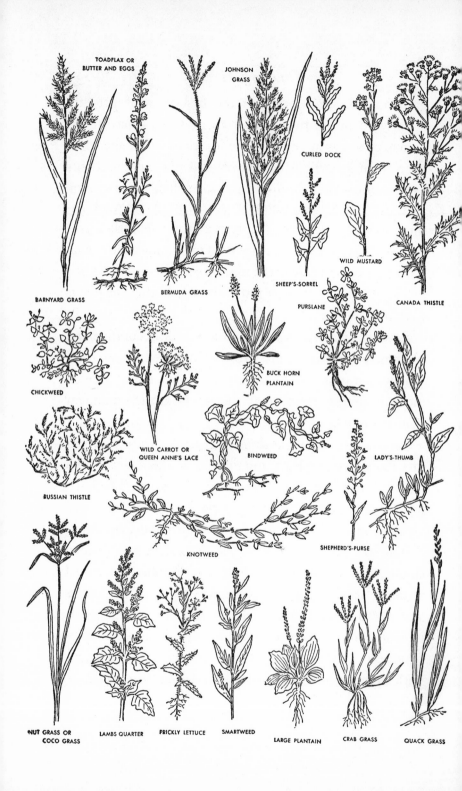

TOADFLAX OR
BUTTER AND EGGS

JOHNSON
GRASS

CURLED DOCK

WILD MUSTARD

SHEEP'S-SORREL

PURSLANE

BARNYARD GRASS

BERMUDA GRASS

CANADA THISTLE

CHICKWEED

BUCK HORN
PLANTAIN

WILD CARROT OR
QUEEN ANNE'S LACE

BINDWEED

LADY'S-THUMB

RUSSIAN THISTLE

KNOTWEED

SHEPHERD'S-PURSE

NUT GRASS OR
COCO GRASS

LAMBS QUARTER

PRICKLY LETTUCE

SMARTWEED

LARGE PLANTAIN

CRAB GRASS

QUACK GRASS

CHAPTER IX

Weeds of the Vegetable Garden

There is some soul of goodness in things evil,
Would men observingly distil it out.
King Henry V, iv.l.

A weed is a plant out of place, an unwanted plant, and many there be that plague the vegetable gardener, much of whose summer time is given to their eradication with scuffle and hoe. Yet they are not all wholly a curse in the garden, since in the work of their destruction the soil is loosened and aerated; nay, some of them are worth picking for use, if taken in their younger days.

Some of the more familiar weeds are listed here for purposes of reference:

Barnyard Grass, *Echinochloa crus-galli:* Intrudes almost everywhere; an annual grass with very plentiful seeds which some of the Indians used to eat.

Bermuda Grass, *Cynodon dactylon:* A coarse perennial of the South, used in places as a lawn grass but a pest in the vegetable garden.

Bindweed, *Convolvulus* spp.: All the bindweeds are difficult to eradicate completely but it must be done.

Wild buckwheat or black bindweed, *Polygonum convolvulus*, is one of the worst of this clan.

CANADA THISTLE, *Cirsium arvense:* Perennial; a thug of a weed that yields only to the spade.

WILD CARROT or QUEEN ANNE'S LACE, *Daucus carota:* The poor but persistent ancestor of the garden carrot. Familiar, but useless.

CHICKWEED, *Stellaria media:* A low-growing and weak-looking but very persistent annual, usually hand-weeded. Quite edible when boiled. Mouse-ear chickweed, *Cerastium vulgatum*, is a relative often found in lawns.

CRAB GRASS, *Digitaria sanguinalis:* The plague of many lawns; often spreads into the vegetable plot. Must be prevented from seeding.

CURLED DOCK, *Rumex crispus:* A deep-rooted, troublesome weed, to be dug out. The leaves are edible if gathered young, parboiled, the water changed, then boiled with a piece of pork.

JOHNSON GRASS, *Holcus halepensis:* A strong grass, very useful in its place, which is the Southern fields, but a noxious weed elsewhere.

KNOTWEED, *Polygonum aviculare:* A creeping, wiry pest of lawn and garden, though it also covers many an ugly spot of bare yard.

LADY'S-THUMB, *Polygonum persicaria:* An erect and bolder cousin of knotweed, easily recognized by the dark mark on the leaves.

Lambs-quarter, *Chenopodium album:* Eminently edible if eaten young, and preferred by some to spinach. Thus those who spurn it by the name of Pigweed are of the baser sort. Its odd name comes from Lammas Quarter, which began with the Loaf Mass to which were brought loaves made from the first wheat of harvest.

Nut Grass or Coco Grass, *Cyperus rotundus:* A pest in many gardens of the South and occasionally in the North, near seaports. The nutlike tubers are edible, though not so good as those of its near relation, the chufa.

Plantain, large, *Plantago major,* and Buckhorn Plantain, *P. lanceolata:* Major pests both, for which no good word can be said. One has broad leaves; the other, narrow; being perennials, they are to be dug out.

Prickly Lettuce, *Lactuca scariola:* Also known as the Compass Plant from its habit of turning its leaves edgewise to the sun. Standing three feet high or higher it looks unlike its cultured descendants in the garden, but the leaves are good either as salad or potherbs when young.

Purslane, *Portulaca oleracea:* Exasperatingly persistent and very spreading. Perhaps the best way to get rid of it would be to cultivate a taste for its mildly acid flavor. Though now but a weed in American gardens, it was cultivated not so long ago—and still is, in Europe.

Quack Grass, *Agropyron repens:* A very difficult pest to eradicate as its white pointed roots must every inch be removed.

RAGWEED, *Ambrosia* spp.: Both the low and the tall ragweeds should be destroyed as soon as recognized, for they cause misery to millions, being the chief irritant in hay fever. Nature abhors a bare spot and ragweed is one of the plants that comes apparently from nowhere to cover it, the reason being its copious production of seeds.

RUSSIAN THISTLE, *Salsola pestifer:* Another of the bare spot coverers, too common in the East and one of the worst pests of the West, but this is understandable, for it is a tumbleweed. Sometimes cooked in the West when very young.

SHEEP'S-SORREL, *Rumex acetosella:* Once this perennial creeper with arrow-shaped leaves is established in a garden, only the most industrious grubbing will overcome it.

SHEPHERD'S-PURSE, *Capsella bursa-pastoris:* One of the mustard tribe and edible either in salad or boiled. Very prolific but easily controlled if kept from seeding.

SMARTWEED, *Polygonum pennsylvanium:* A sprawling weed with little clusters of flowers which result in numerous seeds.

TOADFLAX or BUTTER AND EGGS, *Linaria vulgaris:* Its flowers look like small snapdragons, but it is a difficult pest with long, running rootstocks that will eventually die if the plants are kept cut down.

WILD MUSTARD or CHARLOCK, *Brassica arvensis:* A ubiquitous annual with familiar yellow flowers which should never be allowed to go to seed.

CHAPTER X

Insects and Insecticides

INSECTS

The gardener may consider as marauding intruders those insects that injure his vegetables; but the insects, if they were capable of any such reflection, might deem themselves entitled to take toll from man, a comparative newcomer to the world they inhabited for 500,000,000 years before he appeared upon it.

Insects are so named from the Latin *insectum*, cut in, referring to the often deeply marked division into head, thorax, and abdomen. They are small animals which have six legs at some stage of life, a definition which includes such diverse creatures as aphids and dragonflies, but excludes, for example, spiders, which have eight legs, or pill bugs, which have fourteen.

In numbers insects are by far the most extensive group of animals, averaging perhaps 25,000,000 over each square mile of earth's surface. There are millions of species, and upward of 600,000 have been named and

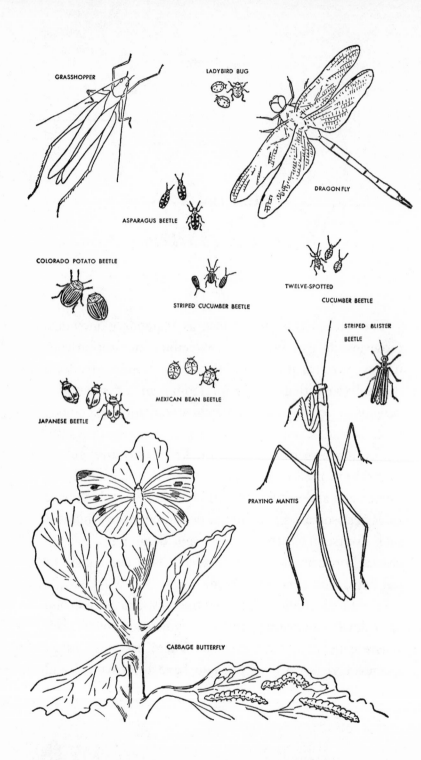

described, of which about 80,000 exist in North America. The majority of these are beneficial, carrying on the all-important work of pollination, assisting in the reduction of decaying plants and animal remains, or preying on harmful species. But the destructive insects cost this country about $2,000,000,000 a year, and war must be unceasingly waged against them.

Insects are different from other animals in many ways besides the possession of six legs. They lack an internal skeleton, and most of them have instead a light, tough exterior coat of chitin (pronounced ky'tin) covering even the eyes. It is resistant to chemicals that would dissolve bones and is one of the reasons why it has been difficult to find an insecticide capable of destroying pests without injuring plants. Many of the soft bodied aphids are protected instead by a waxy, woolly covering.

The blood of insects is yellowish or greenish, not circulated through arteries and veins but drawn in from the general body area to a central tube which forces it to the head, whence it flows back around the body. Instead of lungs, finely branched tracheae open from the sides, and it is through these air tubes that contact poisons attack. Despite the hundreds or thousands of facets in their great eyes, insects are short-sighted and depend chiefly on touch and smell for guidance. They have organs of taste and, in some cases, of hearing.

The term "metamorphosis," meaning change of shape, is applied to the involved process of insect development common to all but a few primitive, wingless species such as aphids and springtails. Complete, four-stage metamorphosis, undergone by beetles, weevils, bees, and most others, includes egg, larva, pupa, and adult. The wormlike larva is not at all similar to the adult, nor is the pupa, a stage of external quiescence in which extraordinary internal changes take place. Crickets, grasshoppers, thrips, and sucking insects in general have simple, three-stage metamorphosis: egg, nymph, and adult, the nymph bearing some, though often remote, resemblance to the adult.

Only in the nymph or larva stage does growth take place, the insect molting several times until full size is reached. On hatching, an insect is said to be in its first instar, after the first molt it is in its second instar, and so on. From the last molt of a nymph the adult emerges; from that of a larva the pupal stage begins.

So rapidly do some insects increase that in the course of a single season the world would be blanketed with them to the suffocation of life but for the checks of birds, fish, toads, parasites, diseases, and other insects.

Man fights his insect enemies by two methods: mechanical and chemical. In the first group are picking, trapping, the destruction of overwintering places, and such recent measures as the inspection of ships, airplanes, and cargoes. In the second group are stomach poisons, of which the arsenical compounds are examples; contact poisons such as rotenone, pyrethrum, and nicotine insecticides, and repellents, including Bordeaux mixture, copper dusts, and naphthalene flakes.

In this expensive war between man and insect, two principles of life guidance are in conflict: individual intelligence versus mass instinct. While some insects can be shown to have traces of intelligence, in the main they are driven by blind, unknowing instinct, each individual identical with its fellows in appearance and behavior. Herein lie both their strength and their weakness.

INSECTICIDES

ROTENONE: For ages past South American Indians have caught fish by damming a stream and throwing into it the pulped roots of plants which paralyzed the fish—an ingenious practice recorded as far back as 1725 by Sir Hans Sloane, the Irish doctor whose books and curios formed the beginning of the British Museum. The plant used in Peru for this purpose and for killing ticks and lice was cubé, an evergreen shrub of the bean family; in the Amazon basin it was timbo.

Only in recent years, however, has attention been focused on this remarkable insecticide of the Indians, following the announcement of its value by a Peruvian scientist who sought a control for ticks on llamas, the Andean beasts of burden. Analysis disclosed that the active principle of the roots is rotenone, $C_{23}H_{22}O_6$, a colorless, odorless, crystalline alkaloid very soluble in chloroform and some other chemicals but almost insoluble in water, toxic to insects and fish but not poisonous to man or his animals—at least in the concentrations of practical use. The crystals or solutions change to yellow, then red, on exposure to light, at the same time becoming less and less toxic. For this reason rotenone insecticides should always be kept in closed, lightproof containers.

Derris, a shrub of the East Indies long known to have insecticidal properties but held suspect because the headhunters of Borneo used it as an ingredient of their poisonous paste for arrowheads, is an important source of rotenone, though in lower percentage than cubé. To the gardener, however, the original source of the rotenone does not matter much, as the dusts obtained by grinding the dried roots are blended to produce a uniform 4 per cent content which, when mixed with spreader material to enable better coverage of the insects, averages .75 of one per cent rotenone in commercial insecticides. This is the concentration that has been found most desirable in dusts. Rotenone 4 per cent sprays are also available, but most gardeners prefer the dust as being more convenient and easy to apply. Lime must never be mixed with derris.

PYRETHRUM: Chief among the other insecticidal materials which do not leave objectional residues on plants is pyrethrum, a powder made from the ground-up flower heads of *Chrysanthemum cinerariaefolium* and kindred species. Formerly imported from abroad due to the high cost of picking the flowers by hand, pyrethrum is now likely to become a commercial crop, following the recent invention of a mechanical picker.

The toxic principles are pyrethrins, which cause paralysis of an insect's nervous system on penetrating the tracheae or breathing tubes. Three forms of the insecticide are in use: powdered flowers, the same mixed with a diluent such as lime or sulphur, and pyrethrum extract, such as the usual 8 per cent kerosene extract of pyrethrum, containing 2½ per cent pyrethrins mixed with 92 per cent diatomaceous earth, the exceedingly fine particles of which are coated with the pyrethrins. This preparation makes the toxic ingredients effective without waste, and they are protected from decomposition by being dissolved in the kerosene.

NICOTINE: The insecticidal principle of tobacco is the alkaloid nicotine, a strong poison which also kills by paralyzing the insect's nervous system, reached via the tracheae. It is most commonly used in the form of nicotine sulphate sold under trade names, such as Black Leaf 40, a nonvolatile preparation which contains 40 per cent nicotine and is mixed at the rate of a teaspoonful to a gallon of water, with about a cubic inch of flake or liquid soap for a spreader, to be used as a spray. Tobacco dust of 2 per cent to 3 per cent nicotine content mixed with slaked lime, sulphur, etc., is also well known.

ARSENICALS: These highly poisonous compounds were formerly in common use against many of the chewing insects but are now being largely replaced by the less dangerous and more satisfactory insecticides above.

Arsenate of lead in particular is no longer considered proper for the garden, as it contains both lead and arsenic. Calcium arsenate is only favored as a spray, with Bordeaux mixture, for potatoes. Paris green, which is copper aceto-arsenite, is still sold as a component of poison bait for cutworms, grasshoppers, etc.

CORROSIVE SUBLIMATE: This is bichloride of mercury, a powerful poison sold in significantly coffin-shaped tablets containing 7.3 grains, one of which in a pint of water gives a 1:1000 solution, used to control the cabbage maggot, disinfect seeds, or treat various stem rots.

COMMON INSECT ENEMIES

APHIDS: All too familiar but nonetheless annoying are the plant lice or aphids, soft-bodied, sap-sucking insects born alive throughout the summer and therefore multiplying with great rapidity. They may be controlled with rotenone dust or nicotine spray, to be applied directly the first specimens are detected.

BLISTER BEETLES: Slender black or striped beetles, formerly used to make blisters because their blood contains an irritant, cantharidin. They feed on leafy vegetables and drop quickly to the ground if alarmed but are easily caught in a can containing kerosene floating on water.

CUTWORMS: Dull-looking, smooth caterpillars of different species of moths which lie hidden by day but emerge at night and cut down young plants, usually at the soil surface. The traditional and effective control is poison bait, to be spread at dusk and cleaned up in the morning lest birds should eat it. The recipe is four ounces of Paris green or white arsenic to five pounds of bran well mixed in one container. In another container half a pint of molasses and the juice of half an orange or lemon are added to two pints of water. Slowly stir this into the poisoned bran until the mash is moist enough to stick together, but not pasty, and let it stand for a couple of hours so that the bran will absorb the poison. Another recipe is chopped clover and Paris green. In either case the poison should not be spread too close to young stems if rain is likely to fall, since the chemicals may be washed around them and injure them.

Alternatively, the stems of young plants may be wrapped with paper, an inch of this to be below the soil surface and two inches above, when they are set out. Where cutworms have been at work they may usually be found afterward curled up near the plant an inch or so below the surface and are often routed out in the course of hoeing. They similarly retire after a meal of the poisoned mash.

FLEA BEETLES: These small insects, which are quite descriptively named, attack cabbage, eggplant, potato, tomato, turnip, and occasionally other vegetables, usually on the underside of the leaves, and may leave them riddled with small holes. Rotenone or nicotine dust gives control.

GRASSHOPPERS: Poisoned bran mash, as for the cutworms, will effectively dispose of grasshoppers also.

JAPANESE BEETLE: This voracious and malefic pest, an iridescent green-and-brown beetle nearly half an inch long, reached New Jersey on a shipment of iris in 1916 and has since then become a very serious menace there and in neighboring states. In its native land, several parasites keep it in control, and some of these have now been introduced by the U.S. Department of Agriculture. Hand picking and rotenone or pyrethrum dusting or spraying are effective where the pests are not too plentiful, as in some afflicted districts where they are shaken from shrubs or trees onto sheets and tipped into pails of kerosene and water. Millions of them have been caught in traps baited with geraniol in a single garden during a summer, but some gardeners think these traps only attract more beetles from adjoining lands. They are undoubtedly effective, however, and cannot fail to reduce the numbers of the succeeding generation.

A nonpoisonous repellent that will keep beetles off beans and other vegetables is made of four ounces of aluminum sulphate and a pound of slaked lime to five gallons of water. When the spray dries a whitish residue is left. Immature silks of corn may be dusted with fine hydrated lime so that they will not be cut by the beetles and pollination prevented.

LEAF HOPPERS: Slender, pale green insects about an eighth of an inch long which feed on the underside of leaves, and hop, scuttle, or fly when disturbed. Nicotine sulphate or rotenone and sulphur dust will give adequate control.

NEMATODES: Microscopic eel-like worms infesting Southern soils and often causing rootknot. Tear gas may control them but in field work they are usually starved out of existence by the planting of resistant species for a few years, such as corn, velvet beans, peanuts and resistant varieties of cowpeas.

RED SPIDER: A tiny mite, about one fiftieth of an inch long, which may infest the underside of bean and other leaves, causing them to wither and fall. Rotenone and sulphur in dust or spray are usually effective.

DISEASES

Plant diseases, other than those due to malnutrition, drought, and unfavorable environment in general, are caused by fungi, bacteria, and viruses.

The fungi which attack vegetables are minute parasitic plants of many species, causing damping-off, mildews, molds, rusts, smuts, etc., on their hosts. They are usually propagated by spores dispersed by wind and germinating only in the presence of moisture.

Bacteria are microscopic plants of great diversity, but only rod-shaped types which multiply by division, not spores, are causal agents of the rots, blights, spots, cankers, etc., with which they afflict garden vegetables. They can be spread only by carriers, which may be raindrops, birds, tools, or many other vehicles.

The causal agent of virus diseases, such as mosaic, yellows, leaf rolling, distortion, and dwarfing, has been the subject of intensive research in recent years. The tobacco virus has been crystallized and has been seen under the electron microscope as a giant rod-shaped molecule attacking green chlorophyll granules. Crystals are not alive, but an exceedingly dilute solution of a virus crystal will infect a plant with disease which spreads like an epidemic. Insects are frequent disseminators of virus infection, and there are other vectors, or carriers, such as the hands or tools that have touched infected plants.

Fortunately these diseases are seldom so serious in vegetable-garden culture as to destroy the crops, but precautions should be taken to prevent their encroachment, for the germs are ubiquitous, borne far by wind, insects, infected seeds or plants, and other means.

Just as with the human body, strong, healthy growth is the best insurance against disease. This implies adequate and suitable plant food; sufficient space for normal development and properly prepared soil through which roots can spread. Such favorable conditions for the vegetables are adverse for the germs of disease, which usually flourish in damp and shady locations, thus there is a double reason for good cultural practices such as drainage, proper plant spacing, and cultivation.

Similarly there is a double reason for keeping preda-tory insects under control since they not only damage the vegetable but may spread diseases. Despite the dust-ing and spraying during the summer, some will survive and go to ground for the winter; fall digging or plow-ing will expose many of them, and garden trash where others may harbor should not be left lying around.

Badly infected plants should be destroyed, and when the disease is one caused by organisms that live in the soil, that particular vegetable should either be grown in an-other part of the garden or abandoned for a few years. Crop rotation is always sound gardening practice.

If serious disease invades the garden and seems beyond the gardener's ability to control, helpful advice may al-ways be had from the plant pathologists of the state agri-cultural experiment station. A full statement of the ap-parent symptoms should be sent and a specimen of the plant, or part of the plant, wrapped in damp moss or other covering that will prevent drying out. But in most cases home treatment, if applied in time, will be effective, and the regular use of a dust combining rotenone and red copper oxide will usually keep down both insects and diseases if the vegetables are healthy and growing in proper environment. Dusts of this type are available at seed stores or may be compounded of such a formula as: Derris 4 per cent rotenone content, three pounds; red copper oxide, one pound; wheat flour, as a sticker, two pounds; talc, as a spreader, fourteen pounds.

In the larger garden, where potatoes, melons, cucumbers, and such large vining crops are grown, Bordeaux mixture is the standard fungicide. This spray takes its name from the vineyards of Bordeaux in France where the value of copper solutions in controlling mildew was discovered about sixty years ago. One of the most commonly used formulas is 4-4-50; that is, four pounds copper sulphate, four pounds hydrated lime, and fifty gallons of water, though 4-2-50 is better for cucumbers and melons which may suffer injury from too much lime.

Bordeaux mixture ready for use may be bought at the stores but is more effective if freshly made. Translating the 4-4-50 formula into terms of garden quantities, four ounces of copper sulphate is dissolved in hot water and added to two gallons of cold water. Four ounces of slaked lime in a gallon of water is then poured into the copper-sulphate solution and stirred well. The mixture is corrosive and should never be left in a metal spray tank or a metal container.

Copper-lime dust, also purchasable at the stores, is less troublesome than Bordeaux mixture, and if applied when plants are wet with rain or dew is practically as effective.

CHAPTER XI

Chemiculture

There is nothing new in the idea of growing plants without soil, as it has long been familiar to scientists, but only in the past few years has it been developed into a practical method for greenhouse culture on a large scale as well as for the few or individual plants grown in homes. Its novelty to the public at large is indicated by the variety of names under which it has been described, as chemiculture, soilless culture, hydroponics, sand culture, tank farming, and water culture.

Among the advantages claimed are control and economy of plant food, saving of labor through the absence of weeds, quicker and greater plant development, and the avoidance of soil-borne diseases and pests. Against these must be set the costs of installation and the attention required, which are high for commercial operation though not deterrent to the home gardener who wishes to try an interesting experiment.

The growth of roots may be seen if a glass bowl or

goldfish tank is used, with wires suspended inside the rim to hold excelsior or peat moss, which will keep the plants upright. The objection to this apparatus is the difficulty of changing or refreshing the water and dissolved plant food in the bowl, which may require a syringe or siphon.

A more practical method is to use a box filled with clean, well-washed, coarse sand, small gravel, or cinders which have been sifted through a half-inch sieve to remove the large pieces and a one-sixteenth-inch mesh, such as a piece of wire window screen, to eliminate dust. Where small seeds are to be sown, it is best to use sand. The box should be waterproofed by painting the inside with asphalt, not tar or paint, and a hole in the bottom is necessary for drainage. It should be covered with a piece of wire screening to prevent the sand from slipping out. The depth of sand or other material will depend on the nature of the plant to be grown, but usually it is five or six inches.

A glazed pot with a hole in the bottom is also a very suitable container. If a metal vessel is used, it should be painted with asphalt to prevent the setting up of chemical action.

Nutrient solution may be prepared by adding to water some of the compounds made for this purpose and sold under various trade names at the stores, or one level teaspoonful each of saltpeter, superphosphate, and epsom salts, with half a teaspoonful of sulphate of ammonia, may be mixed with a gallon of water. This is only one of a number of different formulas that have been worked out. It requires very inexpensive materials and has given good results. Complete commercial fertilizer may be substituted for the saltpeter, superphosphate, and sulphate of ammonia, in which case a level half teaspoonful of the epsom salts should be added per gallon of water.

The amount and frequency of application to the sand box will be governed by the size and nature of the plants. Where seeds have been sown in the sand, it should be merely dampened with plain water until the young plants are about two inches high, when the first drenching of nutrient solution may be given. If this is repeated at intervals of a week, with good sprinklings of plain water between, so as to keep the sand damp, the response of the plants will be the best indication of their requirements. The solution should be freshly made for each application.

Two other methods of supplying the nutrients are in use: the drip method, by which slow drops of the solution are allowed to fall on the sand; and the wick method, by which they are drawn up into the sand from a second container in which the sand box or pot stands. In these methods the supply is small but continuous.

In undrained bowls or tanks the solution should be replaced every three weeks or so and agitated a couple of times a week to aerate it. Whatever method is used, the plants should be allowed as much sunlight as possible.

GREENHOUSE CHEMICULTURE

For tank culture on a large scale in greenhouses, shallow tanks about eight inches deep and as wide as the ordinary greenhouse bench, say two feet, six inches, are made of wood, sheet iron, or concrete covered internally with asphalt. Chicken-wire netting is stretched across the top to support a three-inch layer of excelsior and sawdust, peat moss, or the like, so as to support the growing plants. Horizontal wires are arranged above, to which they may climb.

The space occupied by plants varies with the species, but tomatoes, for example, are grown in two rows allowing each plant one and one quarter square feet of water surface. The tanks are filled to within an inch of the netting at first, but as the roots become longer this air gap is increased. The water is kept circulating so as to aerate it and, when necessary, is warmed by a thermostatically controlled boiler or soil heating cable and is changed every three weeks. The fertilizer solution is added in small amounts at a uniform rate. Huge tomato plants yielding the equivalent of one hundred tons per acre of water surface have been reported raised in California by this method.

Elsewhere sand, gravel, or cinder boxes of greenhouse bench width and as long as desired are watered and fed either from an overhead supply or from a reservoir below the bench with the aid of a pump. This works automatically under the control of a time clock and just barely floods the sand, after which the aqueous solution drains back into the reservoir by gravity.

The prediction has been made that in a mechanized era of the future every housewife will have in her pantry a tank fitted with an artificial sunlight lamp for the production of salad plants. This is an ingenious speculation, but it raises questions as to the nutritional value of foods so grown, and whether the soil may not mean more to plants than an anchorage and a rather wasteful reservoir of inorganic nutrients.

CHAPTER XII

How Plants Live and Grow

Not the least of a gardener's pleasures is his intimate contact with Nature. Like Antaeus, the wrestler of old, who remained undefeated even by the mighty Hercules so long as he could break away from the struggle and renew his strength by touching mother earth, the gardener can forget the worries of his workaday world among the quiet rows of his plants.

When the soil with its teeming life is waked by the sun in spring and he digs to prepare it for the annual miracle of growth, when he sees the expected symmetry of stems and leaves developed from the seeds he has sown, and watches through the season the immemorial drama of the vegetative cycle to its climax, he feels the satisfaction of deep-seated instincts, and is sometimes led to meditative wonder at the processes of plant life.

What is there in a tiny seed that from the soil where it is sown there should arise a stem, and from the stem green leaves put forth, and blossoms come and fruit be borne?

A seed is essentially a miniature plant, exquisitely folded and wrapped for transportation or preservation until it encounters conditions favorable for germination and growth. Food for its first needs is enclosed with it and may be contained in cotyledons, the leaflike organs which beans raise above the soil and peas do not, or may lie adjacent to the embryo plant, as in corn seed.

The seed puts down a rootlet and raises a stem which soon develops leaves. As the rootlet grows it branches and near the tips certain cells elongate outward to form root hairs, through the walls of which soil moisture and dissolved plant food are absorbed and drawn upward through conducting vessels into the leaves. In the leaves is carried on the most important process in the world: the conversion of inorganic materials into organic, whereby the unassimilable elements become food, first for the plant, then for man and beast.

The nature of the process is not fully understood, but we know that from the carbon dioxide of the air and water drawn from the soil, sugar is manufactured and from sugar, starch. These contain only carbon, hydrogen, and oxygen; for the formation of proteins, nitrogen is necessary, and is chiefly derived from the nitrates dissolved in the soil moisture, with the phosphorus, potassium, sulphur, magnesium, calcium, and other elements required in minute quantities for the building of the innumerable and very diverse plant cells.

As circulation proceeds, the foods manufactured in

the leaves are carried to all parts of the plant, and in the case of such vegetables as carrot and turnip much of it moves down to the roots for storage.

The whole structure of the plant, as of all living things, consists of cells, usually microscopic in size, and growth results from the splitting of outer cells, the mechanism being one of fascinating interest.

The vegetables of the garden are seed-bearing plants, though some are propagated in practice by slips or cuttings, and depend on flowers for reproduction. Many of them, however, are biennials and their flowers are not seen in garden culture; in others, notably corn, the flowers are inconspicuous. The male flowers of corn are in the tassel and shed pollen abundantly, as is usually the case when plants depend on wind rather than insects for their distribution. The silks are part of the female flowers and each leads down to an ovule on the cob. A grain of active pollen falling on a receptive silk puts out a little tube which enters the silk and works its way down to the bottom, where an incomplete cell it carries blends with a similarly incomplete ovule cell, each complementing the other so that the union of the two produces a cell which combines characters from both parents. This grows into a kernel or seed, but if such fertilization does not take place, no kernel will be formed, and thus two rows of corn are better in the garden than a single one of twice the length, because of the greater concentration of pollen.

Many plants, on the other hand, produce comparatively small amounts of pollen and display conspicuous, scented, or nectar-bearing flowers to attract insects, which will carry the pollen from one blossom to another, though without any idea, of course, that they are performing such a useful function. Bees are most useful insects in this regard and commercial growers will sometimes put a hive into the middle of a field of cucumbers which without the aid of these industrious workers would probably produce only nubbins and malformed fruits.

Plant breeders make practical use of the various reproductive mechanisms of plants, collecting pollen in bags for transfer to protected female flowers, conveying one blossom by hand into contact with another, enclosing plants or even a row of plants in cheesecloth cages, and introducing flies in the pupa stage at such a time that when they emerge as flies pollen will be shedding and they will carry none from unwanted plants. These are but a few of the devices used in the modern science of plant breeding, which in recent years has so greatly improved the quality of many vegetables that no thoughtful gardener should be content to use a variety merely because his father did so. The lists of progressive seedsmen will well repay study.

APPENDIX

TABLE OF SPRING AND FALL FROST DATES

State	Agricultural Experiment Station	Average date of last frost	Average date of first frost	Days of grow- ing season
Alabama	Gadsden	March 31	Nov. 2	216
	Mobile	Feb. 7	Dec. 5	302
Arizona	Prescott	May 13	Oct. 7	147
	Tucson	March 16	Nov. 20	249
Arkansas	Fayetteville	April 3	Oct. 24	204
	Hope	March 25	Nov. 4	224
California	Chico	March 31	Nov. 20	234
	Santa Monica	Jan. 20	Dec. 26	339
Colorado	Denver	May 10	Oct. 5	148
	Grand Junction	April 20	Oct. 10	173
Connecticut	Hartford	April 20	Oct. 14	177
	New Haven	April 15	Oct. 23	191
Delaware	Newark	April 20	Oct. 17	180
	Dover	April 17	Oct. 23	189
Florida	Jacksonville	Feb. 20	Dec. 1	284
	Tampa	Jan. 15	Dec. 20	339
Georgia	Cornelia	April 15	Oct. 19	187
	Valdosta	March 14	Nov. 11	242
Idaho	Coeur D'Alene	May 12	Oct. 14	155
	Boise	April 28	Oct. 12	167
Illinois	Rockford	May 7	Oct. 11	157
	Anna	April 5	Nov. 1	210
Indiana	South Bend	May 6	Oct. 11	158
	Evansville	April 4	Oct. 27	206
Iowa	Osage	May 10	Sept. 25	138
	Osceola	April 25	Oct. 10	168
Kansas	Leavenworth	April 1	Oct. 18	200
	Winfield	April 15	Oct. 22	190

TABLE OF SPRING AND FALL FROST DATES

State	Agricultural Experiment Station	Average date of last frost	Average date of first frost	Days of grow-ing season
Kentucky	Louisville	April 11	Oct. 22	194
	Paducah	April 7	Oct. 24	200
Louisiana	Shreveport	March 6	Nov. 12	251
	New Orleans	Feb. 18	Dec. 5	290
Maine	Presque Isle	May 31	Sept. 18	110
	Portland	May 5	Oct. 11	159
Maryland	Towson	April 15	Oct. 22	190
	Salisbury	April 20	Oct. 20	183
Massachusetts	Amherst	May 12	Sept. 19	130
	Fall River	April 22	Oct. 23	184
Michigan	Traverse City	May 10	Oct. 9	152
	Detroit	April 29	Oct. 13	167
Minnesota	Two Harbors	May 19	Sept. 27	131
	Worthington	May 10	Sept. 30	143
Mississippi	Tupelo	March 31	Oct. 28	211
	Biloxi	Feb. 22	Nov. 28	279
Missouri	St. Joseph	April 11	Oct. 14	186
	Springfield	April 13	Oct. 20	190
Montana	Moccasin	May 21	Sept. 20	122
	Bozeman	June 1	Sept. 11	102
Nebraska	Alliance	May 12	Sept. 25	136
	Omaha	April 14	Oct. 16	185
Nevada	Lovelock	May 13	Sept. 23	133
	Las Vegas	April 1	Nov. 6	219
New Hampshire	Errol	June 1	Sept. 5	96
	Concord	May 11	Oct. 1	143
New Jersey	Charlotteburg	May 12	Sept. 26	137
	Vineland	April 21	Oct. 20	182
New Mexico	Santa Fe	April 23	Oct. 19	179
	State College	April 9	Oct. 26	200
New York	Buffalo	April 28	Oct. 22	177
	Cutchogue	April 20	Oct. 29	192
North Carolina	Winston-Salem	April 14	Oct. 24	193
	Wilmington	March 22	Nov. 14	237

TABLE OF SPRING AND FALL FROST DATES

State	Agricultural Experiment Station	Average date of last frost		Average date of first frost		Days of grow- ing season
North Dakota	Langdon	June	1	Sept.	12	103
	Fargo	May	20	Sept.	27	130
Ohio	Cleveland	April	16	Nov.	4	202
	Cincinnati	April	9	Oct.	23	197
Oklahoma	Woodward	April	7	Oct.	30	206
	Oklahoma City	March	29	Nov.	4	220
Oregon	Milton	April	17	Oct.	24	190
	Medford	May	7	Oct.	14	160
Pennsylvania	Erie	May	1	Oct.	11	163
	Philadelphia	April	21	Nov.	1	194
Rhode Island	Providence	April	16	Oct.	19	186
	Kingston	May	1	Oct.	14	166
South Carolina	Greenville	March	30	Nov.	6	221
	Charleston	Feb.	20	Dec.	11	294
South Dakota	Aberdeen	May	15	Sept.	23	131
	Yankton	May	2	Oct.	7	158
Tennessee	Cedar Hill	April	9	Oct.	25	199
	Knoxville	April	2	Oct.	29	210
Texas	Lubbock	April	9	Nov.	2	207
	Eagle Pass	Feb.	27	Nov.	26	272
Utah	Salt Lake City	April	20	Oct.	19	182
	St. George	April	19	Oct.	14	178
Vermont	Burlington	April	29	Oct.	8	162
	Bennington	May	15	Oct.	4	142
Virginia	Lynchburg	April	9	Oct.	27	201
	Norfolk	March	25	Nov.	16	236
Washington	Seattle	March	15	Nov.	20	250
	Walla Walla	April	10	Nov.	1	205
West Virginia	Terra Alta	June	8	Sept.	26	110
	Point Pleasant	May	23	Oct.	16	146
Wisconsin	Grantsburg	May	22	Sept.	19	120
	Milwaukee	April	26	Oct.	18	175
Wyoming	Powell	May	18	Sept.	20	125
	Torrington	May	20	Sept.	24	127

Garden Measurements

A square with sides of 208.71 feet, about 69½ yards, would be an acre in area.

The sides of a square half acre would be 147.58 feet, and of a square quarter acre 104.35 feet. A garden 33 × 66 feet is exactly one twentieth of an acre; 50 × 100 feet is approximately one eighth of an acre.

A rod contains 30¼ square yards. A square garden one rod in area would have sides of 16½ feet. An acre contains 160 rods, or 4,840 square yards, or 43,500 square feet.

A cubic yard contains 27 cubic feet; 1,728 cubic inches make a cubic foot, equivalent to 25.7 quarts or 6.4 gallons. A cord of wood is 128 cubic feet.

The standard U.S. bushel is 2,150.42 cubic inches, or about 1¼ cubic feet, equal to 4 pecks, or 8 gallons, or 32 quarts. The English bushel is 2,218.20 cubic inches.

A gallon of water occupies 269 cubic inches and weighs approximately 10 pounds; a cubic foot 62.32 pounds. The standard bushel measure holds 77.6 pounds of water.

To find the cubic contents of a cylinder, multiply the area of the base by the height. The area of a circle is πr^2 or the radius squared and multiplied by 3.1416.

An inch of water over one acre amounts to 23,332 gallons, over an area of 50 × 100 feet, nearly 3,000 gallons.

STATE

AGRICULTURAL EXPERIMENT STATIONS

ALABAMA—Auburn
ALASKA—College
ARIZONA—Tucson
ARKANSAS—Fayetteville
CALIFORNIA—Berkeley
COLORADO—Fort Collins
CONNECTICUT — State Station, New Haven; Storrs Station, Storrs
DELAWARE—Newark
FLORIDA—Gainesville
GEORGIA—State Station, Experiment; Coastal Plain Station, Tifton
HAWAII—Honolulu
IDAHO—Moscow
ILLINOIS—Urbana
INDIANA—Lafayette
IOWA—Ames
KANSAS—Manhattan
KENTUCKY—Lexington
LOUISIANA—Baton Rouge
MAINE—Orono
MARYLAND—College Park
MASSACHUSETTS—Amherst
MICHIGAN—East Lansing
MINNESOTA—University Farm, St. Paul
MISSISSIPPI—State College
MISSOURI—College Station, Columbia; Fruit Station, Mountain Grove
MONTANA—Bozeman

NEBRASKA—Lincoln
NEVADA—Reno
NEW HAMPSHIRE—Durham
NEW JERSEY—New Brunswick
NEW MEXICO—State College
NEW YORK — State Station, Geneva; Cornell Station, Ithaca
NORTH CAROLINA—State College Station, Raleigh
NORTH DAKOTA—State College Station, Fargo
OHIO—Wooster
OKLAHOMA—Stillwater
OREGON—Corvallis
PENNSYLVANIA—State College
PUERTO RICO—Mayaguez
RHODE ISLAND—Kingston
SOUTH CAROLINA—Clemson
SOUTH DAKOTA—Brookings
TENNESSEE—Knoxville
TEXAS—College Station
UTAH—Logan
VERMONT—Burlington
VIRGINIA—College Station, Blacksburg; Truck Station, Norfolk
WASHINGTON—College Station, Pullman; Western Wash. Station, Puyallup
WEST VIRGINIA—Morgantown
WISCONSIN—Madison
WYOMING—Laramie

Vegetables at a Glance

A DIGEST OF THE LEADING VARIETIES FOR HOME USE

BEANS

Variety	Plant	Pod Shape	Pod Color	Seed Color
Asgrow Stringless Tendergreen	Bush	Straight, round	Med. green	Mottled purple
Black Valentine	Bush	Straight, oval	Deep green	Black
Bountiful	Bush	Straight, flat	Light green	Straw
Burpee's Stringless	Bush	Curved, round	Med. green	Coffee-brown
Cornfield	Pole	Straight, round	Med. green	Mottled buff
Decatur	Pole	Near straight	Bright green	Ivory white
French's Hort.	Bush	Straight, broad	Green and carmine	Mottled red
Full Measure	Bush	Straight, round	Med. dark green	Mottled brown
Giant Stringless	Bush	Sl. curved, round	Med. green	Yellowish brown
Golden Wax	Bush	Straight, oval	Waxy yellow	Mottled white
Ideal Market	Pole	Curved, round	Silv'ry green	Black
Kentucky Wonder	Pole	Curved, round	Med. green	Buff
Lazy Wife	Pole	Clusters, oval	Med. green	White
McCaslan	Pole	Curved, thick flat	Med. green	Ivory
Pencil Pod	Bush	Curved, round	Med. yellow	Black
Plentiful	Bush	Straight, flat	Light green	Black
Rd. Pod Kid. Wax	Bush	Sl. curved, round	Med. yellow	White, black eye
Sure Crop	Bush	Straight, thick	Deep yellow	Black
Tenn. Green Pod	Bush	Very large, stringy	Dark green	Med. brown
Wht. Creaseback	Pole	Sl. curved, round	Med. green	Ivory

CABBAGE

Variety	Shape	Diam. Inches	Weight in lb.	Yellows-resistant Strain
All Head	Med. flat	9	6	All Head Select
All Season	Flat globe	9	8	Wisc. All Season
Charleston Wakefield	Conical	6½	4	
Copenhagen Market	Globe	6	3½	Marion Market
Early Flat Dutch	Flat	11	10	
Glory of Enkhuizen	Globe	8	6	Improved Globe
Golden Acre	Globe	6	3	Resist. Gold Acre
Green Acre	Globe	6	3	
Hollander	Globe	7½	6½	Wisc. Hollander
Jersey Wakefield	Conical	5	2½	Jersey Queen
Mammoth Red Rock	Globe	7	7	Red Hollander
Penn. State	Flat globe	7½	5½	
Prem. Late Dutch	Flat	10	8	
Red Dutch	Globe	7	7	
Savoy Perfection	Globe	7	6	
Succession	Flat globe	10	8	

CUCUMBERS

Variety	Use	Spines	Length Inches	Color
A & C	Slicing	White	8½	Dark green
Arlington	Slicing	White	7½	Med. green
Boston Pickling	Pickling	Black	6	Med. green
Chicago Pickling	Pickling	Black	6½	Med. green
Clark's Special	Slicing	White	8	Dark green
Colorado	Slicing	White	8½	Very dark
Early Fortune	Slicing	White	8	Dark green
Gherkin	Pickling	Green	2½	Light green
Lemon	Slicing	Black	3	Lemon
Longfellow	Slicing	White	12	Very dark
Nat. Assn. Pickle	Pickling	Black	6	Dark green
Stays Green	Slicing	White	7	Dark green
Straight-8	Slicing	White	8	Dark green
Woodruff	Slicing	White	8	Dark green

LETTUCE

Variety	Type	Size	Outer Color
Big Boston	Butter head	Medium	Dark green
Grand Rapids	Loose	Large	Light green
Hanson	Cabbage	Large	Yellow green
Iceberg	Cabbage	Large	Light green
Imperial D	Cabbage	Medium	Bright green
Imperial 44	Cabbage	Med. large	Light green
Imperial 152	Cabbage	Med. large	Light green
Imperial 847	Cabbage	Med. large	Med. light green
May Queen	Cabbage	Med. large	Light green
New York	Cabbage	Large	Bright green
New York 12	Cabbage	Large	Lighter than N. Y.
New York 515	Cabbage	Med. large	Brighter than 12
Prize Head	Loose	Medium	Tinged brown
Simpson b. s.	Loose	Large	Light green
Simpson Ey. Curled	Loose	Med. large	Yellow-green
White Boston	Butter head	Medium	Med. green
White Paris	Cos	Med. large	Med. dark green

LIMA BEANS

Variety	Plant	Pod Length Inches	Pod Width Inches	Seeds Size	Seeds Color
Baby Potato	Bush	2¾	¾	Small	Bright green
Burpee Imp'd.	Bush, large	5	1¼	Large	Greenish white
Challenger	Pole	4½	1¼	Large	Pale green
Clark's Bush	Bush, small	2¾	¾	Small	Pale green
Dreer's	Bush, large	3¼	1	Large	Greenish white
Fordhook	Bush, large	4	1	Large	White
Henderson's	Bush, small	2¾	¾	Small	White
Jackson Wonder	Bush	3	¾	Small	Buff, mottled
King of Garden	Pole	6	1¼	Large	White
Sieva } Small White	Pole	3¼	¾	Small	White
Wood's Prolific	Bush	3¼	¾	Small	White

MELONS

Variety	Shape	Size Inches	Exterior	Flesh
Banana	Long	20x4	Lemon	Salmon
Bender's Surprise	Oval	8x7	Deep furrows	Salmon
Fordhook	Oblate	4x5	Netted ribs	Salmon-yel.
Hale's Best	Oval	6x5	Heavy net	Salmon
Hearts of Gold	Globe	6x6	Netted ribs	Pink
Honey Ball	Globe	5x5	Nr. smooth	Green
Honey Dew	Round	7½x7	Smooth	Green
Honey Rock	Globe	5½x5	Coarse net	Salmon
Netted Gem (Rocky Ford)	Round	5½x5	Heavy net	Green
Osage	Oval	7x6	Dark green	Salmon
Perfecto, Impd.	Round	6x5	Medium net	Orange
Pride of Wisconsin	Round	6x5½	Sparse net	Orange
Queen of Colorado	Round	6½x6	Coarse net	Orange
Tip Top	Oval	7x6	Slight ribs	Salmon

ONIONS

Variety	Shape	Exterior Color	Notes
Australian Brown	Flat globe	Brown	Strong flavor
Brigham Yellow Globe	Globe	Yellow	Good keeper
Crystal Wax	Flat	White	For S. W.
Early Yellow Globe	Globe	Rich yellow	Good keeper
Ebenezer	Deep flat	Dk. yellow	For good sets
Golden Globe	Long globe	Rich yellow	Good for sets
Nebuka	Bunching	White	Does not bulb
Prizetaker	Large globe	Lt. yellow	Thin skin
Red Wethersfield	Deep flat	Purple red	For sets and storage
Southport Red Globe	Globe	Purple red	The best red
Southport White Globe	Globe	White	The best white
Southport Yellow Globe	Globe	Orange yellow	Good keeper
Sweet Spanish Yellow	Globe	Amber gold	Large size
White Portugal	Thick flat	White	Pickles and bunching
Yellow Danvers Globe	Globe	Med. yellow	Standard variety
Yellow Strassburg	Flat	Yellow	Hardy, keeps well

PEAS

Variety	Season	Plant		Pod			Similar Strains
		Inches	Color	Shape	Color	Inches	
Alaska*	1st Early	28	Light	Blunt	Light	2½	
Alderman*	Main	50	Dark	Pointed	Dark	4½	Telephone
Amer. Wonder	Early	12	Dark	Blunt	Light	2½	
Dwf. Telephone*	Late	24	Light	Pointed	Light	4½	
Everbearing*	Late	28	Dark	Blunt	Light	3	⎧ No. 40.
Giant Stride*	Late	26	Dark	Pointed	Dark	4¾	⎨ Icer.
Gilbo*	Main	26	Dark	Pointed	Dark	4½	⎩ Wy. Wonder.
Gradus	Early	32	Med.	Pointed	Med.	4	
Hundredfold	Early	20	Dark	Pointed	Dark	4	
Laxtonian	Early	16	Dark	Pointed	Dark	4¼	
Lax's. Progress	Early	15	Dark	Pointed	Dark	4½	
Lax's. Superb	Early	17	Light	Pointed	Med.	4	Early Bird
Little Marvel	Early	18	Dark	Blunt	Dark	3	
Marrowfat Wh.*	Late	50	Med.	Blunt	Light	3	
Morse's Market	Main	26	Med.	Pointed	Dark	4½	
Nott's Excelsior	Early	15	Dark	Blunt	Light	2¾	
Pedigree*	1st Early	26	Light	Blunt	Light	2½	First & Best
Premium Gem*	Early	22	Dark	Blunt	Light	2¾	
Stratagem	Late	26	Dark	Pointed	Dark	4½	
Teton*	Main	32	Dark	Blunt	Dark	3¾	
Thomas Laxton	Early	34	Dark	Blunt	Dark	3½	
World's Record	Early	24	Light	Pointed	Med.	3½	

*Resistant to Fusarium wilt.

PEPPERS

Variety	Flavor	Length Inches	Diam. Inches	Shape
California Wonder	Sweet	4½	3½	Oblong
Cayenne	Very hot	5	¾	Long pointed
Chinese Giant	Sweet	4½	4½	Square
Early Giant	Sweet	4½	3½	Nr. square
Hungarian Yellow	Pungent	6	1½	Long pointed
Paprika	Mostly sweet	4	1¼	Tapered
Pimento	Sweet	3¼	2¼	Heart
Red Chili	Very hot	2	½	Tapered
Ruby King	Sweet	5	3	Tapered
Squash (Tomato)	Sweet	1½	2¼	Tomato
Tabasco	Hot	1	½	Tapered
World Beater	Sweet	5	3½	Oblong

RADISHES

Variety	Season	Outer Color	Shape
Cavalier	Spring	Scarlet	Olive
China Rose	Winter	Bright red	Oblong, 5″ long
China White	Winter	White	Oblong, 8″ long
Crimson Giant	Spring	Deep crimson	Turnip, 1½″ diam.
Early Scarlet Globe	Spring	Scarlet	Olive to globe
French Breakfast	Spring	Scarlet, white tip	Oblong, 1½″ long
Icicle	Summer	White	Tapered, 5″ long
Long Scarlet	Summer	Deep scarlet	Tapered, 5″ long
Scarlet Turnip white-tipped	Spring	Scarlet, white tip	Turnip, 1″ diam.
Spanish Long	Winter	Black	Cylindrical, 8″ long
Spanish Round	Winter	Black	Turnip, 3″ diam.
Sparkler	Spring	Scarlet, white tip	Near globe, 1½″ diam.
White Strasburg	Summer	White	Tapered, 5″ long

SWEET CORN

Variety	Season	Ears			Stalk in Feet
		Color	Length Inches	Rows	
Bantam Evergreen	Late	Yellow	8	14–18	7
Black Mexican	Main	White	8	8	7
Charlevoix	Main	Yellow	6½	10–12	5½
Country Gentleman	Late	White	7½	Zig-zag	7
Early Market	Early	White	6	10–12	4½
Golden Bantam	Main	Yellow	6	8	5
Golden Cross Bantam*	Main	Yellow	8	12–14	6½
Golden Early Market	Early	Yellow	7	10–14	4½
Honey June	Late	White	8	12–16	8
Howling Mob	Main	White	7½	12–16	7
Ioana*	Main	Yellow	7½	12–14	7
Marcross*	Early	Yellow	7	12–16	5
Spancross*	Early	Yellow	6½	10–14	5½
Stowell's Evergreen	Late	White	9	16–18	8
Tendergold*	Main	Yellow	7½	12–14	6
Whipple's Early Yellow	Main	Yellow	7	12–16	6

*A hybrid variety.

TOMATOES

Variety	Season	Shape	Color	Size
Bonny Best	Main	Oblate	Red	Med. large
Break o' Day	Early	Globe	Red	Medium
Clark's Early	Early	Oblate	Red	Medium
Earliana	Early	Fl. globe	Red	Medium
Golden Queen	Late	Deep flat	Yellow	Large
Greater Baltimore	Main	Flat	Red	Large
Grothen's Globe	Early	Globe	Red	Medium
Gulf State Mkt.	Main	Globe	Pink	Med. large
June Pink	Early	Fl. globe	Pink	Medium
Livingston's Globe	Main	Globe	Pink	Large
Marglobe	Main	Globe	Red	Med. large
Mingold	Main	Globe	Yellow	Med. large
Oxheart	Late	Heart	Pink	Large
Ponderosa	Late	Flat	Pink	V. large
Pritchard	Main	Nr. globe	Red	Medium
Rutgers	Main	Globe	Red	Medium
Scarlet Dawn	Early	Globe	Red	Med. large
Stokesdale	Early	Globe	Red	Med. large
Stone	Late	Deep flat	Red	Large

INDEX

A CATALOGUE OF SELECTED DOVER BOOKS
IN ALL FIELDS OF INTEREST

A CATALOGUE OF SELECTED DOVER BOOKS
IN ALL FIELDS OF INTEREST

AMERICA'S OLD MASTERS, James T. Flexner. Four men emerged unexpectedly from provincial 18th century America to leadership in European art: Benjamin West, J. S. Copley, C. R. Peale, Gilbert Stuart. Brilliant coverage of lives and contributions. Revised, 1967 edition. 69 plates. 365pp. of text.

21806-6 Paperbound $3.00

FIRST FLOWERS OF OUR WILDERNESS: AMERICAN PAINTING, THE COLONIAL PERIOD, James T. Flexner. Painters, and regional painting traditions from earliest Colonial times up to the emergence of Copley, West and Peale Sr., Foster, Gustavus Hesselius, Feke, John Smibert and many anonymous painters in the primitive manner. Engaging presentation, with 162 illustrations. xxii + 368pp.

22180-6 Paperbound $3.50

THE LIGHT OF DISTANT SKIES: AMERICAN PAINTING, 1760-1835, James T. Flexner. The great generation of early American painters goes to Europe to learn and to teach: West, Copley, Gilbert Stuart and others. Allston, Trumbull, Morse; also contemporary American painters—primitives, derivatives, academics—who remained in America. 102 illustrations. xiii + 306pp.   22179-2 Paperbound $3.50

A HISTORY OF THE RISE AND PROGRESS OF THE ARTS OF DESIGN IN THE UNITED STATES, William Dunlap. Much the richest mine of information on early American painters, sculptors, architects, engravers, miniaturists, etc. The only source of information for scores of artists, the major primary source for many others. Unabridged reprint of rare original 1834 edition, with new introduction by James T. Flexner, and 394 new illustrations. Edited by Rita Weiss. 6⅝ x 9⅝.

21695-0, 21696-9, 21697-7 Three volumes, Paperbound $13.50

EPOCHS OF CHINESE AND JAPANESE ART, Ernest F. Fenollosa. From primitive Chinese art to the 20th century, thorough history, explanation of every important art period and form, including Japanese woodcuts; main stress on China and Japan, but Tibet, Korea also included. Still unexcelled for its detailed, rich coverage of cultural background, aesthetic elements, diffusion studies, particularly of the historical period. 2nd, 1913 edition. 242 illustrations. lii + 439pp. of text.

20364-6, 20365-4 Two volumes, Paperbound $6.00

THE GENTLE ART OF MAKING ENEMIES, James A. M. Whistler. Greatest wit of his day deflates Oscar Wilde, Ruskin, Swinburne; strikes back at inane critics, exhibitions, art journalism; aesthetics of impressionist revolution in most striking form. Highly readable classic by great painter. Reproduction of edition designed by Whistler. Introduction by Alfred Werner. xxxvi + 334pp.

21875-9 Paperbound $3.00

VISUAL ILLUSIONS: THEIR CAUSES, CHARACTERISTICS, AND APPLICATIONS, Matthew Luckiesh. Thorough description and discussion of optical illusion, geometric and perspective, particularly; size and shape distortions, illusions of color, of motion; natural illusions; use of illusion in art and magic, industry, etc. Most useful today with op art, also for classical art. Scores of effects illustrated. Introduction by William H. Ittleson. 100 illustrations. xxi + 252pp.

21530-X Paperbound $2.00

A HANDBOOK OF ANATOMY FOR ART STUDENTS, Arthur Thomson. Thorough, virtually exhaustive coverage of skeletal structure, musculature, etc. Full text, supplemented by anatomical diagrams and drawings and by photographs of undraped figures. Unique in its comparison of male and female forms, pointing out differences of contour, texture, form. 211 figures, 40 drawings, 86 photographs. xx + 459pp. 5⅜ x 8⅜.

21163-0 Paperbound $3.50

150 MASTERPIECES OF DRAWING, Selected by Anthony Toney. Full page reproductions of drawings from the early 16th to the end of the 18th century, all beautifully reproduced: Rembrandt, Michelangelo, Dürer, Fragonard, Urs, Graf, Wouwerman, many others. First-rate browsing book, model book for artists. xviii + 150pp. 8⅜ x 11¼.

21032-4 Paperbound' $2.50

THE LATER WORK OF AUBREY BEARDSLEY, Aubrey Beardsley. Exotic, erotic, ironic masterpieces in full maturity: Comedy Ballet, Venus and Tannhauser, Pierrot, Lysistrata, Rape of the Lock, Savoy material, Ali Baba, Volpone, etc. This material revolutionized the art world, and is still powerful, fresh, brilliant. With *The Early Work*, all Beardsley's finest work. 174 plates, 2 in color. xiv + 176pp. 8⅛ x 11.

21817-1 Paperbound $3.00

DRAWINGS OF REMBRANDT, Rembrandt van Rijn. Complete reproduction of fabulously rare edition by Lippmann and Hofstede de Groot, completely reedited, updated, improved by Prof. Seymour Slive, Fogg Museum. Portraits, Biblical sketches, landscapes, Oriental types, nudes, episodes from classical mythology—All Rembrandt's fertile genius. Also selection of drawings by his pupils and followers. "Stunning volumes," *Saturday Review*. 550 illustrations. lxxviii + 552pp. 9⅛ x 12¼.

21485-0, 21486-9 Two volumes, Paperbound $10.00

THE DISASTERS OF WAR, Francisco Goya. One of the masterpieces of Western civilization—83 etchings that record Goya's shattering, bitter reaction to the Napoleonic war that swept through Spain after the insurrection of 1808 and to war in general. Reprint of the first edition, with three additional plates from Boston's Museum of Fine Arts. All plates facsimile size. Introduction by Philip Hofer, Fogg Museum. v + 97pp. 9⅜ x 8¼.

21872-4 Paperbound $2.00

GRAPHIC WORKS OF ODILON REDON. Largest collection of Redon's graphic works ever assembled: 172 lithographs, 28 etchings and engravings, 9 drawings. These include some of his most famous works. All the plates from *Odilon Redon: oeuvre graphique complet*, plus additional plates. New introduction and caption translations by Alfred Werner. 209 illustrations. xxvii + 209pp. 9⅛ x 12¼.

21966-8 Paperbound $4.00

DESIGN BY ACCIDENT; A BOOK OF "ACCIDENTAL EFFECTS" FOR ARTISTS AND DESIGNERS, James F. O'Brien. Create your own unique, striking, imaginative effects by "controlled accident" interaction of materials: paints and lacquers, oil and water based paints, splatter, crackling materials, shatter, similar items. Everything you do will be different; first book on this limitless art, so useful to both fine artist and commercial artist. Full instructions. 192 plates showing "accidents," 8 in color. viii + 215pp. 8⅜ x 11¼. 21942-9 Paperbound $3.50

THE BOOK OF SIGNS, Rudolf Koch. Famed German type designer draws 493 beautiful symbols: religious, mystical, alchemical, imperial, property marks, runes, etc. Remarkable fusion of traditional and modern. Good for suggestions of timelessness, smartness, modernity. Text. vi + 104pp. 6⅛ x 9¼. 20162-7 Paperbound $1.25

HISTORY OF INDIAN AND INDONESIAN ART, Ananda K. Coomaraswamy. An unabridged republication of one of the finest books by a great scholar in Eastern art. Rich in descriptive material, history, social backgrounds; Sunga reliefs, Rajput paintings, Gupta temples, Burmese frescoes, textiles, jewelry, sculpture, etc. 400 photos. viii + 423pp. 6⅜ x 9¾. 21436-2 Paperbound $5.00

PRIMITIVE ART, Franz Boas. America's foremost anthropologist surveys textiles, ceramics, woodcarving, basketry, metalwork, etc.; patterns, technology, creation of symbols, style origins. All areas of world, but very full on Northwest Coast Indians. More than 350 illustrations of baskets, boxes, totem poles, weapons, etc. 378 pp. 20025-6 Paperbound $3.00

THE GENTLEMAN AND CABINET MAKER'S DIRECTOR, Thomas Chippendale. Full reprint (third edition, 1762) of most influential furniture book of all time, by master cabinetmaker. 200 plates, illustrating chairs, sofas, mirrors, tables, cabinets, plus 24 photographs of surviving pieces. Biographical introduction by N. Bienenstock. vi + 249pp. 9⅞ x 12¾. 21601-2 Paperbound $4.00

AMERICAN ANTIQUE FURNITURE, Edgar G. Miller, Jr. The basic coverage of all American furniture before 1840. Individual chapters cover type of furniture—clocks, tables, sideboards, etc.—chronologically, with inexhaustible wealth of data. More than 2100 photographs, all identified, commented on. Essential to all early American collectors. Introduction by H. E. Keyes. vi + 1106pp. 7⅞ x 10¾. 21599-7, 21600-4 Two volumes, Paperbound $11.00

PENNSYLVANIA DUTCH AMERICAN FOLK ART, Henry J. Kauffman. 279 photos, 28 drawings of tulipware, Fraktur script, painted tinware, toys, flowered furniture, quilts, samplers, hex signs, house interiors, etc. Full descriptive text. Excellent for tourist, rewarding for designer, collector. Map. 146pp. 7⅞ x 10¾. 21205-X Paperbound $2.50

EARLY NEW ENGLAND GRAVESTONE RUBBINGS, Edmund V. Gillon, Jr. 43 photographs, 226 carefully reproduced rubbings show heavily symbolic, sometimes macabre early gravestones, up to early 19th century. Remarkable early American primitive art, occasionally strikingly beautiful; always powerful. Text. xxvi + 207pp. 8⅜ x 11¼. 21380-3 Paperbound $3.50

ALPHABETS AND ORNAMENTS, Ernst Lehner. Well-known pictorial source for decorative alphabets, script examples, cartouches, frames, decorative title pages, calligraphic initials, borders, similar material. 14th to 19th century, mostly European. Useful in almost any graphic arts designing, varied styles. 750 illustrations. 256pp. 7 x 10.   21905-4 Paperbound $4.00

PAINTING: A CREATIVE APPROACH, Norman Colquhoun. For the beginner simple guide provides an instructive approach to painting: major stumbling blocks for beginner; overcoming them, technical points; paints and pigments; oil painting; watercolor and other media and color. New section on "plastic" paints. Glossary. Formerly *Paint Your Own Pictures*. 221pp.   22000-1 Paperbound $1.75

THE ENJOYMENT AND USE OF COLOR, Walter Sargent. Explanation of the relations between colors themselves and between colors in nature and art, including hundreds of little-known facts about color values, intensities, effects of high and low illumination, complementary colors. Many practical hints for painters, references to great masters. 7 color plates, 29 illustrations. x + 274pp.
20944-X Paperbound $2.75

THE NOTEBOOKS OF LEONARDO DA VINCI, compiled and edited by Jean Paul Richter. 1566 extracts from original manuscripts reveal the full range of Leonardo's versatile genius: all his writings on painting, sculpture, architecture, anatomy, astronomy, geography, topography, physiology, mining, music, etc., in both Italian and English, with 186 plates of manuscript pages and more than 500 additional drawings. Includes studies for the Last Supper, the lost Sforza monument, and other works. Total of xlvii + 866pp. 7⅞ x 10¾.
22572-0, 22573-9 Two volumes, Paperbound $10.00

MONTGOMERY WARD CATALOGUE OF 1895. Tea gowns, yards of flannel and pillow-case lace, stereoscopes, books of gospel hymns, the New Improved Singer Sewing Machine, side saddles, milk skimmers, straight-edged razors, high-button shoes, spittoons, and on and on . . . listing some 25,000 items, practically all illustrated. Essential to the shoppers of the 1890's, it is our truest record of the spirit of the period. Unaltered reprint of Issue No. 57, Spring and Summer 1895. Introduction by Boris Emmet. Innumerable illustrations. xiii + 624pp. 8½ x 11⅝.
22377-9 Paperbound $6.95

THE CRYSTAL PALACE EXHIBITION ILLUSTRATED CATALOGUE (LONDON, 1851). One of the wonders of the modern world—the Crystal Palace Exhibition in which all the nations of the civilized world exhibited their achievements in the arts and sciences—presented in an equally important illustrated catalogue. More than 1700 items pictured with accompanying text—ceramics, textiles, cast-iron work, carpets, pianos, sleds, razors, wall-papers, billiard tables, beehives, silverware and hundreds of other artifacts—represent the focal point of Victorian culture in the Western World. Probably the largest collection of Victorian decorative art ever assembled— indispensable for antiquarians and designers. Unabridged republication of the Art-Journal Catalogue of the Great Exhibition of 1851, with all terminal essays. New introduction by John Gloag, F.S.A. xxxiv + 426pp. 9 x 12.
22503-8 Paperbound $5.00

A History of Costume, Carl Köhler. Definitive history, based on surviving pieces of clothing primarily, and paintings, statues, etc. secondarily. Highly readable text, supplemented by 594 illustrations of costumes of the ancient Mediterranean peoples, Greece and Rome, the Teutonic prehistoric period; costumes of the Middle Ages, Renaissance, Baroque, 18th and 19th centuries. Clear, measured patterns are provided for many clothing articles. Approach is practical throughout. Enlarged by Emma von Sichart. 464pp. 21030-8 Paperbound $3.50.

Oriental Rugs, Antique and Modern, Walter A. Hawley. A complete and authoritative treatise on the Oriental rug—where they are made, by whom and how, designs and symbols, characteristics in detail of the six major groups, how to distinguish them and how to buy them. Detailed technical data is provided on periods, weaves, warps, wefts, textures, sides, ends and knots, although no technical background is required for an understanding. 11 color plates, 80 halftones, 4 maps. vi + 320pp. $6\frac{1}{8}$ x $9\frac{1}{8}$. 22366-3 Paperbound $5.00

Ten Books on Architecture, Vitruvius. By any standards the most important book on architecture ever written. Early Roman discussion of aesthetics of building, construction methods, orders, sites, and every other aspect of architecture has inspired, instructed architecture for about 2,000 years. Stands behind Palladio, Michelangelo, Bramante, Wren, countless others. Definitive Morris H. Morgan translation. 68 illustrations. xii + 331pp. 20645-9 Paperbound $3.00

The Four Books of Architecture, Andrea Palladio. Translated into every major Western European language in the two centuries following its publication in 1570, this has been one of the most influential books in the history of architecture. Complete reprint of the 1738 Isaac Ware edition. New introduction by Adolf Placzek, Columbia Univ. 216 plates. xxii + 110pp. of text. $9\frac{1}{2}$ x $12\frac{3}{4}$. 21308-0 Clothbound $10.00

Sticks and Stones: A Study of American Architecture and Civilization, Lewis Mumford.One of the great classics of American cultural history. American architecture from the medieval-inspired earliest forms to the early 20th century; evolution of structure and style, and reciprocal influences on environment. 21 photographic illustrations. 238pp. 20202-X Paperbound $2.00

The American Builder's Companion, Asher Benjamin. The most widely used early 19th century architectural style and source book, for colonial up into Greek Revival periods. Extensive development of geometry of carpentering, construction of sashes, frames, doors, stairs; plans and elevations of domestic and other buildings. Hundreds of thousands of houses were built according to this book, now invaluable to historians, architects, restorers, etc. 1827 edition. 59 plates. 114pp. $7\frac{7}{8}$ x $10\frac{3}{4}$. 22236-5 Paperbound $3.50

Dutch Houses in the Hudson Valley Before 1776, Helen Wilkinson Reynolds. The standard survey of the Dutch colonial house and outbuildings, with constructional features, decoration, and local history associated with individual homesteads. Introduction by Franklin D. Roosevelt. Map. 150 illustrations. 469pp. $6\frac{5}{8}$ x $9\frac{1}{4}$. 21469-9 Paperbound

THE ARCHITECTURE OF COUNTRY HOUSES, Andrew J. Downing. Together with Vaux's *Villas and Cottages* this is the basic book for Hudson River Gothic architecture of the middle Victorian period. Full, sound discussions of general aspects of housing, architecture, style, decoration, furnishing, together with scores of detailed house plans, illustrations of specific buildings, accompanied by full text. Perhaps the most influential single American architectural book. 1850 edition. Introduction by J. Stewart Johnson. 321 figures, 34 architectural designs. xvi + 560pp.
22003-6 Paperbound $4.00

LOST EXAMPLES OF COLONIAL ARCHITECTURE, John Mead Howells. Full-page photographs of buildings that have disappeared or been so altered as to be denatured, including many designed by major early American architects. 245 plates. xvii + 248pp. 7⅞ x 10¾.
21143-6 Paperbound $3.50

DOMESTIC ARCHITECTURE OF THE AMERICAN COLONIES AND OF THE EARLY REPUBLIC, Fiske Kimball. Foremost architect and restorer of Williamsburg and Monticello covers nearly 200 homes between 1620-1825. Architectural details, construction, style features, special fixtures, floor plans, etc. Generally considered finest work in its area. 219 illustrations of houses, doorways, windows, capital mantels. xx + 314pp. 7⅞ x 10¾.
21743-4 Paperbound $4.00

EARLY AMERICAN ROOMS: 1650-1858, edited by Russell Hawes Kettell. Tour of 12 rooms, each representative of a different era in American history and each furnished, decorated, designed and occupied in the style of the era. 72 plans and elevations, 8-page color section, etc., show fabrics, wall papers, arrangements, etc. Full descriptive text. xvii + 200pp. of text. 8⅜ x 11¼.
21633-0 Paperbound $5.00

THE FITZWILLIAM VIRGINAL BOOK, edited by J. Fuller Maitland and W. B. Squire. Full modern printing of famous early 17th-century ms. volume of 300 works by Morley, Byrd, Bull, Gibbons, etc. For piano or other modern keyboard instrument; easy to read format. xxxvi + 938pp. 8⅜ x 11.
21068-5, 21069-3 Two volumes, Paperbound $10.00

KEYBOARD MUSIC, Johann Sebastian Bach. Bach Gesellschaft edition. A rich selection of Bach's masterpieces for the harpsichord: the six English Suites, six French Suites, the six Partitas (Clavierübung part I), the Goldberg Variations (Clavierübung part IV), the fifteen Two-Part Inventions and the fifteen Three-Part Sinfonias. Clearly reproduced on large sheets with ample margins; eminently playable. vi + 312pp. 8⅛ x 11.
22360-4 Paperbound $5.00

THE MUSIC OF BACH: AN INTRODUCTION, Charles Sanford Terry. A fine, nontechnical introduction to Bach's music, both instrumental and vocal. Covers organ music, chamber music, passion music, other types. Analyzes themes, developments, innovations. x + 114pp.
21075-8 Paperbound $1.50

BEETHOVEN AND HIS NINE SYMPHONIES, Sir George Grove. Noted British musicologist provides best history, analysis, commentary on symphonies. Very thorough, rigorously accurate; necessary to both advanced student and amateur music lover. 436 musical passages. vii + 407 pp.
20334-4 Paperbound $2.75

JOHANN SEBASTIAN BACH, Philipp Spitta. One of the great classics of musicology, this definitive analysis of Bach's music (and life) has never been surpassed. Lucid, nontechnical analyses of hundreds of pieces (30 pages devoted to St. Matthew Passion, 26 to B Minor Mass). Also includes major analysis of 18th-century music. 450 musical examples. 40-page musical supplement. Total of xx + 1799pp.

(EUK) 22278-0, 22279-9 Two volumes, Clothbound $17.50

MOZART AND HIS PIANO CONCERTOS, Cuthbert Girdlestone. The only full-length study of an important area of Mozart's creativity. Provides detailed analyses of all 23 concertos, traces inspirational sources. 417 musical examples. Second edition. 509pp.

21271-8 Paperbound $3.50

THE PERFECT WAGNERITE: A COMMENTARY ON THE NIBLUNG'S RING, George Bernard Shaw. Brilliant and still relevant criticism in remarkable essays on Wagner's Ring cycle, Shaw's ideas on political and social ideology behind the plots, role of Leitmotifs, vocal requisites, etc. Prefaces. xxi + 136pp.

(USO) 21707-8 Paperbound $1.50

DON GIOVANNI, W. A. Mozart. Complete libretto, modern English translation; biographies of composer and librettist; accounts of early performances and critical reaction. Lavishly illustrated. All the material you need to understand and appreciate this great work. Dover Opera Guide and Libretto Series; translated and introduced by Ellen Bleiler. 92 illustrations. 209pp.

21134-7 Paperbound $2.00

BASIC ELECTRICITY, U. S. Bureau of Naval Personel. Originally a training course, best non-technical coverage of basic theory of electricity and its applications. Fundamental concepts, batteries, circuits, conductors and wiring techniques, AC and DC, inductance and capacitance, generators, motors, transformers, magnetic amplifiers, synchros, servomechanisms, etc. Also covers blue-prints, electrical diagrams, etc. Many questions, with answers. 349 illustrations. x + 448pp. $6\frac{1}{2}$ x $9\frac{1}{4}$.

20973-3 Paperbound $3.50

REPRODUCTION OF SOUND, Edgar Villchur. Thorough coverage for laymen of high fidelity systems, reproducing systems in general, needles, amplifiers, preamps, loudspeakers, feedback, explaining physical background. "A rare talent for making technicalities vividly comprehensible," R. Darrell, *High Fidelity*. 69 figures. iv + 92pp.

21515-6 Paperbound $1.25

HEAR ME TALKIN' TO YA: THE STORY OF JAZZ AS TOLD BY THE MEN WHO MADE IT, Nat Shapiro and Nat Hentoff. Louis Armstrong, Fats Waller, Jo Jones, Clarence Williams, Billy Holiday, Duke Ellington, Jelly Roll Morton and dozens of other jazz greats tell how it was in Chicago's South Side, New Orleans, depression Harlem and the modern West Coast as jazz was born and grew. xvi + 429pp.

21726-4 Paperbound $3.00

FABLES OF AESOP, translated by Sir Roger L'Estrange. A reproduction of the very rare 1931 Paris edition; a selection of the most interesting fables, together with 50 imaginative drawings by Alexander Calder. v + 128pp. $6\frac{1}{2}$x$9\frac{1}{4}$.

21780-9 Paperbound $1.50

AGAINST THE GRAIN (A REBOURS), Joris K. Huysmans. Filled with weird images, evidences of a bizarre imagination, exotic experiments with hallucinatory drugs, rich tastes and smells and the diversions of its sybarite hero Duc Jean des Esseintes, this classic novel pushed 19th-century literary decadence to its limits. Full unabridged edition. Do not confuse this with abridged editions generally sold. Introduction by Havelock Ellis. xlix + 206pp. 22190-3 Paperbound $2.00

VARIORUM SHAKESPEARE: HAMLET. Edited by Horace H. Furness; a landmark of American scholarship. Exhaustive footnotes and appendices treat all doubtful words and phrases, as well as suggested critical emendations throughout the play's history. First volume contains editor's own text, collated with all Quartos and Folios. Second volume contains full first Quarto, translations of Shakespeare's sources (Belleforest, and Saxo Grammaticus), Der Bestrafte Brudermord, and many essays on critical and historical points of interest by major authorities of past and present. Includes details of staging and costuming over the years. By far the best edition available for serious students of Shakespeare. Total of xx + 905pp. 21004-9, 21005-7, 2 volumes, Paperbound $7.00

A LIFE OF WILLIAM SHAKESPEARE, Sir Sidney Lee. This is the standard life of Shakespeare, summarizing everything known about Shakespeare and his plays. Incredibly rich in material, broad in coverage, clear and judicious, it has served thousands as the best introduction to Shakespeare. 1931 edition. 9 plates. xxix + 792pp. (USO) 21967-4 Paperbound $3.75

MASTERS OF THE DRAMA, John Gassner. Most comprehensive history of the drama in print, covering every tradition from Greeks to modern Europe and America, including India, Far East, etc. Covers more than 800 dramatists, 2000 plays, with biographical material, plot summaries, theatre history, criticism, etc. "Best of its kind in English," *New Republic*. 77 illustrations. xxii + 890pp. 20100-7 Clothbound $8.50

THE EVOLUTION OF THE ENGLISH LANGUAGE, George McKnight. The growth of English, from the 14th century to the present. Unusual, non-technical account presents basic information in very interesting form: sound shifts, change in grammar and syntax, vocabulary growth, similar topics. Abundantly illustrated with quotations. Formerly *Modern English in the Making*. xii + 590pp. 21932-1 Paperbound $3.50

AN ETYMOLOGICAL DICTIONARY OF MODERN ENGLISH, Ernest Weekley. Fullest, richest work of its sort, by foremost British lexicographer. Detailed word histories, including many colloquial and archaic words; extensive quotations. Do not confuse this with the Concise Etymological Dictionary, which is much abridged. Total of xxvii + 830pp. 6½ x 9¼. 21873-2, 21874-0 Two volumes, Paperbound $7.90

FLATLAND: A ROMANCE OF MANY DIMENSIONS, E. A. Abbott. Classic of science-fiction explores ramifications of life in a two-dimensional world, and what happens when a three-dimensional being intrudes. Amusing reading, but also useful as introduction to thought about hyperspace. Introduction by Banesh Hoffmann. 16 illustrations. xx + 103pp. 20001-9 Paperbound $1.00

POEMS OF ANNE BRADSTREET, edited with an introduction by Robert Hutchinson. A new selection of poems by America's first poet and perhaps the first significant woman poet in the English language. 48 poems display her development in works of considerable variety—love poems, domestic poems, religious meditations, formal elegies, "quaternions," etc. Notes, bibliography. viii + 222pp.
22160-1 Paperbound $2.50

THREE GOTHIC NOVELS: THE CASTLE OF OTRANTO BY HORACE WALPOLE; VATHEK BY WILLIAM BECKFORD; THE VAMPYRE BY JOHN POLIDORI, WITH FRAGMENT OF A NOVEL BY LORD BYRON, edited by E. F. Bleiler. The first Gothic novel, by Walpole; the finest Oriental tale in English, by Beckford; powerful Romantic supernatural story in versions by Polidori and Byron. All extremely important in history of literature; all still exciting, packed with supernatural thrills, ghosts, haunted castles, magic, etc. xl + 291pp.
21232-7 Paperbound $2.50

THE BEST TALES OF HOFFMANN, E. T. A. Hoffmann. 10 of Hoffmann's most important stories, in modern re-editings of standard translations: Nutcracker and the King of Mice, Signor Formica, Automata, The Sandman, Rath Krespel, The Golden Flowerpot, Master Martin the Cooper, The Mines of Falun, The King's Betrothed, A New Year's Eve Adventure. 7 illustrations by Hoffmann. Edited by E. F. Bleiler. xxxix + 419pp.
21793-0 Paperbound $3.00

GHOST AND HORROR STORIES OF AMBROSE BIERCE, Ambrose Bierce. 23 strikingly modern stories of the horrors latent in the human mind: The Eyes of the Panther, The Damned Thing, An Occurrence at Owl Creek Bridge, An Inhabitant of Carcosa, etc., plus the dream-essay, Visions of the Night. Edited by E. F. Bleiler. xxii + 199pp.
20767-6 Paperbound $1.50

BEST GHOST STORIES OF J. S. LeFANU, J. Sheridan LeFanu. Finest stories by Victorian master often considered greatest supernatural writer of all. Carmilla, Green Tea, The Haunted Baronet, The Familiar, and 12 others. Most never before available in the U. S. A. Edited by E. F. Bleiler. 8 illustrations from Victorian publications. xvii + 467pp.
20415-4 Paperbound $3.00

MATHEMATICAL FOUNDATIONS OF INFORMATION THEORY, A. I. Khinchin. Comprehensive introduction to work of Shannon, McMillan, Feinstein and Khinchin, placing these investigations on a rigorous mathematical basis. Covers entropy concept in probability theory, uniqueness theorem, Shannon's inequality, ergodic sources, the E property, martingale concept, noise, Feinstein's fundamental lemma, Shanon's first and second theorems. Translated by R. A. Silverman and M. D. Friedman. iii + 120pp.
60434-9 Paperbound $1.75

SEVEN SCIENCE FICTION NOVELS, H. G. Wells. The standard collection of the great novels. Complete, unabridged. *First Men in the Moon, Island of Dr. Moreau, War of the Worlds, Food of the Gods, Invisible Man, Time Machine, In the Days of the Comet.* Not only science fiction fans, but every educated person owes it to himself to read these novels. 1015pp. (USO) 20264-X Clothbound $6.00

LAST AND FIRST MEN AND STAR MAKER, TWO SCIENCE FICTION NOVELS, Olaf Stapledon. Greatest future histories in science fiction. In the first, human intelligence is the "hero," through strange paths of evolution, interplanetary invasions, incredible technologies, near extinctions and reemergences. Star Maker describes the quest of a band of star rovers for intelligence itself, through time and space: weird inhuman civilizations, crustacean minds, symbiotic worlds, etc. Complete, unabridged. v + 438pp. (USO) 21962-3 Paperbound $2.50

THREE PROPHETIC NOVELS, H. G. WELLS. Stages of a consistently planned future for mankind. *When the Sleeper Wakes,* and *A Story of the Days to Come,* anticipate *Brave New World* and *1984,* in the 21st Century; *The Time Machine,* only complete version in print, shows farther future and the end of mankind. All show Wells's greatest gifts as storyteller and novelist. Edited by E. F. Bleiler. x + 335pp. (USO) 20605-X Paperbound $2.50

THE DEVIL'S DICTIONARY, Ambrose Bierce. America's own Oscar Wilde—Ambrose Bierce—offers his barbed iconoclastic wisdom in over 1,000 definitions hailed by H. L. Mencken as "some of the most gorgeous witticisms in the English language." 145pp. 20487-1 Paperbound $1.25

MAX AND MORITZ, Wilhelm Busch. Great children's classic, father of comic strip, of two bad boys, Max and Moritz. Also Ker and Plunk (Plisch und Plumm), Cat and Mouse, Deceitful Henry, Ice-Peter, The Boy and the Pipe, and five other pieces. Original German, with English translation. Edited by H. Arthur Klein; translations by various hands and H. Arthur Klein. vi + 216pp. 20181-3 Paperbound $2.00

PIGS IS PIGS AND OTHER FAVORITES, Ellis Parker Butler. The title story is one of the best humor short stories, as Mike Flannery obfuscates biology and English. Also included, That Pup of Murchison's, The Great American Pie Company, and Perkins of Portland. 14 illustrations. v + 109pp. 21532-6 Paperbound $1.25

THE PETERKIN PAPERS, Lucretia P. Hale. It takes genius to be as stupidly mad as the Peterkins, as they decide to become wise, celebrate the "Fourth," keep a cow, and otherwise strain the resources of the Lady from Philadelphia. Basic book of American humor. 153 illustrations. 219pp. 20794-3 Paperbound $1.50

PERRAULT'S FAIRY TALES, translated by A. E. Johnson and S. R. Littlewood, with 34 full-page illustrations by Gustave Doré. All the original Perrault stories—Cinderella, Sleeping Beauty, Bluebeard, Little Red Riding Hood, Puss in Boots, Tom Thumb, etc.—with their witty verse morals and the magnificent illustrations of Doré. One of the five or six great books of European fairy tales. viii + 117pp. 8⅛ x 11. 22311-6 Paperbound $2.00

OLD HUNGARIAN FAIRY TALES, Baroness Orczy. Favorites translated and adapted by author of the *Scarlet Pimpernel.* Eight fairy tales include "The Suitors of Princess Fire-Fly," "The Twin Hunchbacks," "Mr. Cuttlefish's Love Story," and "The Enchanted Cat." This little volume of magic and adventure will captivate children as it has for generations. 90 drawings by Montagu Barstow. 96pp. 22293-4 Paperbound $1.95

THE RED FAIRY BOOK, Andrew Lang. Lang's color fairy books have long been children's favorites. This volume includes Rapunzel, Jack and the Bean-stalk and 35 other stories, familiar and unfamiliar. 4 plates, 93 illustrations x + 367pp.
21673-X Paperbound $2.50

THE BLUE FAIRY BOOK, Andrew Lang. Lang's tales come from all countries and all times. Here are 37 tales from Grimm, the Arabian Nights, Greek Mythology, and other fascinating sources. 8 plates, 130 illustrations. xi + 390pp.
21437-0 Paperbound $2.50

HOUSEHOLD STORIES BY THE BROTHERS GRIMM. Classic English-language edition of the well-known tales — Rumpelstiltskin, Snow White, Hansel and Gretel, The Twelve Brothers, Faithful John, Rapunzel, Tom Thumb (52 stories in all). Translated into simple, straightforward English by Lucy Crane. Ornamented with headpieces, vignettes, elaborate decorative initials and a dozen full-page illustrations by Walter Crane. x + 269pp.
21080-4 Paperbound $2.00

THE MERRY ADVENTURES OF ROBIN HOOD, Howard Pyle. The finest modern versions of the traditional ballads and tales about the great English outlaw. Howard Pyle's complete prose version, with every word, every illustration of the first edition. Do not confuse this facsimile of the original (1883) with modern editions that change text or illustrations. 23 plates plus many page decorations. xxii + 296pp.
22043-5 Paperbound $2.50

THE STORY OF KING ARTHUR AND HIS KNIGHTS, Howard Pyle. The finest children's version of the life of King Arthur; brilliantly retold by Pyle, with 48 of his most imaginative illustrations. xviii + 313pp. 6⅛ x 9¼.
21445-1 Paperbound $2.50

THE WONDERFUL WIZARD OF OZ, L. Frank Baum. America's finest children's book in facsimile of first edition with all Denslow illustrations in full color. The edition a child should have. Introduction by Martin Gardner. 23 color plates, scores of drawings. iv + 267pp.
20691-2 Paperbound $2.50

THE MARVELOUS LAND OF OZ, L. Frank Baum. The second Oz book, every bit as imaginative as the Wizard. The hero is a boy named Tip, but the Scarecrow and the Tin Woodman are back, as is the Oz magic. 16 color plates, 120 drawings by John R. Neill. 287pp.
20692-0 Paperbound $2.50

THE MAGICAL MONARCH OF MO, L. Frank Baum. Remarkable adventures in a land even stranger than Oz. The best of Baum's books not in the Oz series. 15 color plates and dozens of drawings by Frank Verbeck. xviii + 237pp.
21892-9 Paperbound $2.25

THE BAD CHILD'S BOOK OF BEASTS, MORE BEASTS FOR WORSE CHILDREN, A MORAL ALPHABET, Hilaire Belloc. Three complete humor classics in one volume. Be kind to the frog, and do not call him names . . . and 28 other whimsical animals. Familiar favorites and some not so well known. Illustrated by Basil Blackwell. 156pp.
(USO) 20749-8 Paperbound $1.50

EAST O' THE SUN AND WEST O' THE MOON, George W. Dasent. Considered the best of all translations of these Norwegian folk tales, this collection has been enjoyed by generations of children (and folklorists too). Includes True and Untrue, Why the Sea is Salt, East O' the Sun and West O' the Moon, Why the Bear is Stumpy-Tailed, Boots and the Troll, The Cock and the Hen, Rich Peter the Pedlar, and 52 more. The only edition with all 59 tales. 77 illustrations by Erik Werenskiold and Theodor Kittelsen. xv + 418pp. 22521-6 Paperbound $3.50

GOOPS AND HOW TO BE THEM, Gelett Burgess. Classic of tongue-in-cheek humor, masquerading as etiquette book. 87 verses, twice as many cartoons, show mischievous Goops as they demonstrate to children virtues of table manners, neatness, courtesy, etc. Favorite for generations. viii + 88pp. 6½ x 9¼. 22233-0 Paperbound $1.25

ALICE'S ADVENTURES UNDER GROUND, Lewis Carroll. The first version, quite different from the final *Alice in Wonderland,* printed out by Carroll himself with his own illustrations. Complete facsimile of the "million dollar" manuscript Carroll gave to Alice Liddell in 1864. Introduction by Martin Gardner. viii + 96pp. Title and dedication pages in color. 21482-6 Paperbound $1.25

THE BROWNIES, THEIR BOOK, Palmer Cox. Small as mice, cunning as foxes, exuberant and full of mischief, the Brownies go to the zoo, toy shop, seashore, circus, etc., in 24 verse adventures and 266 illustrations. Long a favorite, since their first appearance in St. Nicholas Magazine. xi + 144pp. 6⅝ x 9¼. 21265-3 Paperbound $1.75

SONGS OF CHILDHOOD, Walter De La Mare. Published (under the pseudonym Walter Ramal) when De La Mare was only 29, this charming collection has long been a favorite children's book. A facsimile of the first edition in paper, the 47 poems capture the simplicity of the nursery rhyme and the ballad, including such lyrics as I Met Eve, Tartary, The Silver Penny. vii + 106pp. (USO) 21972-0 Paperbound $1.25

THE COMPLETE NONSENSE OF EDWARD LEAR, Edward Lear. The finest 19th-century humorist-cartoonist in full: all nonsense limericks, zany alphabets, Owl and Pussycat, songs, nonsense botany, and more than 500 illustrations by Lear himself. Edited by Holbrook Jackson. xxix + 287pp. (USO) 20167-8 Paperbound $2.00

BILLY WHISKERS: THE AUTOBIOGRAPHY OF A GOAT, Frances Trego Montgomery. A favorite of children since the early 20th century, here are the escapades of that rambunctious, irresistible and mischievous goat—Billy Whiskers. Much in the spirit of *Peck's Bad Boy,* this is a book that children never tire of reading or hearing. All the original familiar illustrations by W. H. Fry are included: 6 color plates, 18 black and white drawings. 159pp. 22345-0 Paperbound $2.00

MOTHER GOOSE MELODIES. Faithful republication of the fabulously rare Munroe and Francis "copyright 1833" Boston edition—the most important Mother Goose collection, usually referred to as the "original." Familiar rhymes plus many rare ones, with wonderful old woodcut illustrations. Edited by E. F. Bleiler. 128pp. 4½ x 6⅜. 22577-1 Paperbound $1.00

TWO LITTLE SAVAGES; BEING THE ADVENTURES OF TWO BOYS WHO LIVED AS INDIANS AND WHAT THEY LEARNED, Ernest Thompson Seton. Great classic of nature and boyhood provides a vast range of woodlore in most palatable form, a genuinely entertaining story. Two farm boys build a teepee in woods and live in it for a month, working out Indian solutions to living problems, star lore, birds and animals, plants, etc. 293 illustrations. vii + 286pp.

20985-7 Paperbound $2.50

PETER PIPER'S PRACTICAL PRINCIPLES OF PLAIN & PERFECT PRONUNCIATION. Alliterative jingles and tongue-twisters of surprising charm, that made their first appearance in America about 1830. Republished in full with the spirited woodcut illustrations from this earliest American edition. 32pp. 4½ x 6⅜.

22560-7 Paperbound $1.00

SCIENCE EXPERIMENTS AND AMUSEMENTS FOR CHILDREN, Charles Vivian. 73 easy experiments, requiring only materials found at home or easily available, such as candles, coins, steel wool, etc.; illustrate basic phenomena like vacuum, simple chemical reaction, etc. All safe. Modern, well-planned. Formerly *Science Games for Children*. 102 photos, numerous drawings. 96pp. 6⅛ x 9¼.

21856-2 Paperbound $1.25

AN INTRODUCTION TO CHESS MOVES AND TACTICS SIMPLY EXPLAINED, Leonard Barden. Informal intermediate introduction, quite strong in explaining reasons for moves. Covers basic material, tactics, important openings, traps, positional play in middle game, end game. Attempts to isolate patterns and recurrent configurations. Formerly *Chess*. 58 figures. 102pp. (USO) 21210-6 Paperbound $1.25

LASKER'S MANUAL OF CHESS, Dr. Emanuel Lasker. Lasker was not only one of the five great World Champions, he was also one of the ablest expositors, theorists, and analysts. In many ways, his Manual, permeated with his philosophy of battle, filled with keen insights, is one of the greatest works ever written on chess. Filled with analyzed games by the great players. A single-volume library that will profit almost any chess player, beginner or master. 308 diagrams. xli X 349pp.

20640-8 Paperbound $2.75

THE MASTER BOOK OF MATHEMATICAL RECREATIONS, Fred Schuh. In opinion of many the finest work ever prepared on mathematical puzzles, stunts, recreations; exhaustively thorough explanations of mathematics involved, analysis of effects, citation of puzzles and games. Mathematics involved is elementary. Translated by F. Göbel. 194 figures. xxiv + 430pp. 22134-2 Paperbound $3.50

MATHEMATICS, MAGIC AND MYSTERY, Martin Gardner. Puzzle editor for Scientific American explains mathematics behind various mystifying tricks: card tricks, stage "mind reading," coin and match tricks, counting out games, geometric dissections, etc. Probability sets, theory of numbers clearly explained. Also provides more than 400 tricks, guaranteed to work, that you can do. 135 illustrations. xii + 176pp.

20335-2 Paperbound $1.75

MATHEMATICAL PUZZLES FOR BEGINNERS AND ENTHUSIASTS, Geoffrey Mott-Smith. 189 puzzles from easy to difficult—involving arithmetic, logic, algebra, properties of digits, probability, etc.—for enjoyment and mental stimulus. Explanation of mathematical principles behind the puzzles. 135 illustrations. viii + 248pp.
20198-8 Paperbound $1.75

PAPER FOLDING FOR BEGINNERS, William D. Murray and Francis J. Rigney. Easiest book on the market, clearest instructions on making interesting, beautiful origami. Sail boats, cups, roosters, frogs that move legs, bonbon boxes, standing birds, etc. 40 projects; more than 275 diagrams and photographs. 94pp.
20713-7 Paperbound $1.00

TRICKS AND GAMES ON THE POOL TABLE, Fred Herrmann. 79 tricks and games—some solitaires, some for two or more players, some competitive games—to entertain you between formal games. Mystifying shots and throws, unusual caroms, tricks involving such props as cork, coins, a hat, etc. Formerly *Fun on the Pool Table*. 77 figures. 95pp.
21814-7 Paperbound $1.00

HAND SHADOWS TO BE THROWN UPON THE WALL: A SERIES OF NOVEL AND AMUSING FIGURES FORMED BY THE HAND, Henry Bursill. Delightful picturebook from great-grandfather's day shows how to make 18 different hand shadows: a bird that flies, duck that quacks, dog that wags his tail, camel, goose, deer, boy, turtle, etc. Only book of its sort. vi + 33pp. 6½ x 9¼.
21779-5 Paperbound $1.00

WHITTLING AND WOODCARVING, E. J. Tangerman. 18th printing of best book on market. "If you can cut a potato you can carve" toys and puzzles, chains, chessmen, caricatures, masks, frames, woodcut blocks, surface patterns, much more. Information on tools, woods, techniques. Also goes into serious wood sculpture from Middle Ages to present, East and West. 464 photos, figures. x + 293pp.
20965-2 Paperbound $2.00

HISTORY OF PHILOSOPHY, Julián Marías. Possibly the clearest, most easily followed, best planned, most useful one-volume history of philosophy on the market; neither skimpy nor overfull. Full details on system of every major philosopher and dozens of less important thinkers from pre-Socratics up to Existentialism and later. Strong on many European figures usually omitted. Has gone through dozens of editions in Europe. 1966 edition, translated by Stanley Appelbaum and Clarence Strowbridge. xviii + 505pp.
21739-6 Paperbound $3.50

YOGA: A SCIENTIFIC EVALUATION, Kovoor T. Behanan. Scientific but non-technical study of physiological results of yoga exercises; done under auspices of Yale U. Relations to Indian thought, to psychoanalysis, etc. 16 photos. xxiii + 270pp.
20505-3 Paperbound $2.50

Prices subject to change without notice.
Available at your book dealer or write for free catalogue to Dept. GI, Dover Publications, Inc., 180 Varick St., N. Y., N. Y. 10014. Dover publishes more than 150 books each year on science, elementary and advanced mathematics, biology, music, art, literary history, social sciences and other areas.